I0487796

How To Invest By Instinct

How To Invest By Instinct

Instinctively Self Guided Investments

Lin Eldridge

Writers Club Press
San Jose New York Lincoln Shanghai

How To Invest By Instinct
Instinctively Self Guided Investments

All Rights Reserved © 2001 by LIN eldridge

No part of this book may be reproduced or transmitted in any
form or by any means, graphic, electronic, or mechanical,
including photocopying, recording, taping, or by any
information storage retrieval system, without the
permission in writing from the publisher.

Writers Club Press
an imprint of iUniverse.com, Inc.

For information address:
iUniverse.com, Inc.
5220 S 16th, Ste. 200
Lincoln, NE 68512
www.iuniverse.com

Trading can be hazardous to your pocketbook. Use common sense.

ISBN: 0-595-19533-4

Printed in the United States of America

To my children, Hunter and Tiffany, and family.

Contents

Preface

The (Instinctive) Nature of Christmas
'Twas the night before Christmas and all through the land
instinctive nature was wreaking the devilish hand.
'Tis a season when we're stressed and need to be understood
for time is the asset we would buy if we could.
'Tis a time to spend with family and friends
even if they are driving you to your very wits end.
"Why do these people behave as they do?"
Their instinctive nature will lend us a clue.
"The tree is too tall for the living room ceiling,"
but those high in Create know with what they are dealing.
"Of course it will fit," is the look on their faces
for they can fit objects into the tiniest of spaces.
Those high in Seek will speak of times past
with memories of details that is unusually vast.
to traditions they hold when it's time to prepare
a feast to behold for all their kin to share.
Those high in Order will have everything planned,
for disorder and chaos they cannot stand.
They will shop from lists in an orderly way
and have time left over to relax or to play.
Those high in Invent will deliberate
and will not show till 'tis almost too late.
"You'll never finish," drives this one to complete
for they're most creative when there are deadlines to meet.
So if perchance during this holiday season
you find yourself agitated with no apparent reason,

remember there are reasons we behave as we do,
understanding instinctive nature will help see you through.
For we must realize the power of people to give
peace, harmony and love, which we all need to live.

Acknowledgements

Shaindell Goldhaber, who did a "ghost" of a job processing my words.

To my brokers and market buddies, who since 1969 have helped, hindered and had fun—we both learned and made money.

Alex at Alex Brown

Jim Healy—A.G. Edwards

Mike Bradley

Bruce at Cowan

Eric and Jody—Presidential

Fred Wynia—Sherwood

Don Delong—Rauscher

Laura—Freeman

Buck—Herzog

Dick Bowman—Hambrecht

John Waller

Randy L.—Montgomery

Kevin and Ed—Merrill

Mason—Gruntal

Jerry—OPCO

Peter Marin—O'NEILL

Phil M.—Paine Webber

Tom B and Dean H.—Kidder

Pete Rhinhart—Smith Barney

Wibs—Strom, Susskind

Larry Williams

Tom O'Malley—Forman

Linda Raschke

If you weren't listed, you weren't forgotten—the list had to end somewhere.

Introduction

Dear Reader,

Anybody can trade stocks, but to succeed handsomely over the long haul, one had best have a plan. There are more fund managers of various risks and styles than ever before, with probably over $100 billion collectively under management.

These professionals and successful individuals have one tenet in common, their systematic plan which is personally formatted to their own volition (their choice of intuition, analysis, order (risk rules and discipline) or creativity.

In choosing a personal instinctive investment doctrine one should know one's weaknesses and strengths. These choices should be natural and not forced. They should be matched to risk and return tolerances which are inherent in each individual.

My book, *How to Invest by Instinct*, puts you in charge of your strong suits and allows you to overcome your emotional or other weaknesses by teaching you who you are, your instinctive nature and how best to proceed with your personal investment strategy.

This book is based on the Humanagement tm Test John Furey 602 9528711 Humanagement tm through the use of their proprietary Personal Options Profile tm helps you realize your power and weakness through simple questions and answers in the form of the Humanagement Test. Your Personal Options Profile will define and allow you to develop a balanced investment style based on your personal choices (VOLITIONAL) personal profile and tolerances.

I wrote this book because, after taking the Humanagement Test, I learned my strength (a priori-intuition) and was shocked by my weakness (low in order and rules), this increased my confidence and performance results and also made me feel more in control, since I was "going with the flow" of what was natural for me, my instinctive nature.

Good trading!

— Lin Eldridge

Chapter 1

Profitable Trading

To trade profitably one must possess introspection, to know yourself you will know your limits.

To trade profitably *after knowing yourself* you must believe in yourself. Confidence!

Finally, one must work with *perseverance* in studying with courage and spirit to embark and carry out your plan.

Interaction of introspection, confidence and perseverance are powerful and inlay an intuitive trading mentality.

The traders' mentality is the product of their trading method plus money management and psychology.

There is no magic to trading. I *know* anyone can trade profitably, and that self-acceptance, self-knowledge and belief in oneself are necessary to begin the struggle with trading. And I know it takes both trust and courage to continue that struggle.

Pearl Buck said: "The truly creative mind in any field is no more than this: a human creature born abnormally, inhumanly sensitive. To him a touch is a blow, a sound is a noise, a misfortune is a tragedy, a joy is an ecstasy, a friend is a lover, a lover is a god, and failure is death. Add to this unusually delicate organism the overpowering necessity to create, create, create – so that without the creating of music or poetry or books or buildings or something of meaning, his very breath is cut off from him. He must create, must point out creation. By some strange, unknown inward urgency, he is not really alive unless he is creating."

To me the truly serious successful trader is not fully alive unless he is trading. Also, the good trade pickers have strength to change as the rules of the game change. They adopt the mindset that the market is always right.

Chapter 2

Discipline (Order)

Most of us have trouble with discipline. Those of us who have taken the Humanagement Test know if this is an issue. I certainly know it is a major issue with me (see my profile). Part of order is patience, persistence and lack of stubbornness.

Nothing takes the place of persistence. Not talent, not genius or education. The world is full of geniuses who are in essence educated derelicts. Persistence and determination alone are omnipotent!

When looking at ones rules, and I *could not* trade without my personal *written* rules. One of the reasons I needed to write them is because I am low in discipline (order). I needed to specifically drum into my head, like a jackhammer, to take small losses. Persistence, therefore, is a central theme to rule keeping. It is beyond faith. It is simply "doing it anyway." I like this better than Nike's "Just Do It!"

Part of order is commitment—to oneself, to the dream (goal) of being financially independent. This takes perseverance to be successful. You aren't given the dream without the power of making the dream come true. Your power comes from the willingness to go the extra yard to make your goal reality. That takes commitment. Results determine commitment, not the other way around. Look at what you are actually accomplishing to determine what you are committed to. I use three computers for quotes, charts, analysis, accounting, etc. I post my trades daily using Quicken—I get daily results! I achieve better results than my New Years Annual Financial Goals because I am persistently pursuing my committed goals *daily*. You'd be amazed how much better one does when they say, "I want to make X per year," and then they see that takes Y monthly, and Z daily. Z is the key!

Z is the key!

Chapter 3

Trial and Error

You learn by doing, by experiencing, then fixing it if necessary, but always learning something in the process. The markets are like days and nights (never the same). One needs to adjust to the nuances that line up to produce successful results. First you do it anyway (take the trade!). Then correct it if your results aren't positive. All my life I've taken this approach to learning and thought I was wrong. I wasn't! Trial and error does work. The errors are not wasted either because there is something learned from each trial and each error. When a trade is carried at a loss it is like a hangman's noose. Do you want to cut the noose and stay alive or hang (lose more)? Trading successfully evolves and becomes intuitively second nature. The research which comes from errors makes the discerning differences in validating the correct approach. One can learn from errors by asking what did I learn from this loss? The answer is very stabilizing if one will listen to where they went wrong. This will validate a correct natural selection process. My failures (what didn't work) were much more powerful learning experiences than trades that succeeded! This is a prevalent concept which spills over into personal relationships and all other acts of life.

Chapter 4

Do You Know How to Grow $$?

1. Know what you want to do—i.e. I want to trade a certain way; i.e. methodology, time frame, loss protection, rules, trading rules, analysis and components of trading plan.
2. Set monetary goals—i.e. I want to make X today, Y tomorrow, Z this month and 300X's for the year.
3. *Compost* 1 + 2 above, turning these ideas over and over in your mind.
4. *Ferment* and rake 1 + 2 above.
5. *Digest* 1 + 2 above.
6. *Fertilize* 1+ 2 above with knowledge gained from recent research and trading results (profits and losses).
7. Take in the sun—enjoy the benefits of the gains and learn from the losses.
8. Use all 8 rules above and wait for the green $ to grow!

Chapter 5

Market Strengths

You can control yourself. Also, you can know yourself and predict yourself. The market can be observed, it cannot be controlled. Since you are predictable and the market is not, the dilemma is what to do if the market moves 1, 2 or 3 standard deviations up or down or stays unchanged! It has become apparent to me over the years that is imperative to spend less time looking and following markets and maximum time developing style, rules, trading journals, discipline, systems and strategy. This last sentence is seductive and should be re-read. It is why knowing yourself is the key to your trading strategy.

Although trading is very much a here-and-now action, knowing how to release the past and use it appropriately in the present can be very beneficial. Knowing how to capitalize on the past and "day-dream" into the future can provide creative shortcuts for trading as well. In imagining various situations one could possibly encounter, one can playact out various scenarios and place themselves in the quarterback pocket. This allows us to live and think the trades without the emotions, so when we are in real action we will be more proactive.

To trade is an active verb. Thinking is not trading. Trading is transactions with other partners, both being at risk. Trade out of commitment to your values, rules and commitments to yourself as a trader. Trust yourself!

Oh, if only one could be the proverbial fly o the wall, watching and listening, our puzzled expressions would change to comprehension.

Chapter 6

Tracking an Idea

Right-brain/left-brain research is fascinating, controversial and extremely complex. My own opinion is based on my experience of over 30 years of trading all markets. I relate how I completed two oil paintings, the first a copy of a Monet "Three Ladies Fishing in a Boat," which I gave to my daughter who is into order and doing things correctly. The fact that she hung it on her bedroom wall was like a bold star for me. Another painting, which was theoretical and abstract, I gave to my son. it also was "Art." I mention this because I was switched repeatedly from natural left to right handed in writing class by Catholic nuns and persevered with my left hand. I was told by everyone, especially my father, that my writing was abominable—how could I draw let alone paint? Without any formal education, I know for me it is instinctual that my brain handled the demand input, "I want to oil paint." From there it went emotional. My sensory input of images and colors and intuition synthesized my fantasy.

The markets can also be visual, sensory and highly emotional as well as intellectual, judgmental, rational analytical reality, conceptual and focused. The markets, like art, are composed of the combined input of all buyers and sellers. Left-brain-dominant traders should put their rational/critical self aside, and let themselves go intuitively loose.

The right-brain-dominant group should build by breaking down the research elements and facts, focusing on detail, which allows them to develop a sense of discrimination between what makes sense and what is extraneous, weigh the facts and conclude XYZ is a "Buy/Hold or Sell."

Great traders need both right and left-brain competence. Successful traders do this on instinct, unconsciously. They develop this process to the level where there is a free flow between the use of their left and right brain.

I used to feel frustrated because I couldn't understand how it was that I knew the principles of successful trading intellectually, yet couldn't produce profits which reflected that knowledge. I thought something was wrong with me or the markets! Then I realized there is usually a time gap between my intellectual perception of a fundamental idea and the markets pervasive reaction to the valuation process. I became more technical when I learned I could go with my gut and trusted the feeling (precision and fluidity became integrated). When right and left brains work together there is an easy back and forth process of refinement. Better results come for me when the two sides work in harmony with each other. Idea + Intuition = Trade. I also feed energy into the idea-finger-paint with the thoughts.

Chapter 7

Collaborating with the subconscious

Traders say "I see a pattern developing" or "the trade is setting up" as a way of explaining the source of their inspiration. Experiencing, feeling and seeing are the essence of the right brain's influence.

Another way of "seeing" involves letting go. For some this is familiar, for others a foreign country. Letting go is a random, uncommitted approach (it is like walking on a beach you have never visited before). Nothing to do but enjoy the sun. Walk and view what unfolds. Often when I view my four monitors and am hiking looking for an idea instead of being on my feet, I am on my eyes. What to do? Each symbol conjures up rules, but letting go involves mellowing out. I keep searching until something grabs me (I remind myself I am on a random walk). I usually do this twice each opening. it allows me to cover ground, looking for both longs and shorts. This allows me to collaborate with my subconscious. Try this, it is like experiencing creativity. It allows you to consciously seek out what has been explored unconsciously. The subconscious walk should be without adhering to a time schedule (timelessness) being absorbed in the doing, spontaneous, no sense of outcome, full of observance and non-judgmental, nondiscriminating. All is equal.

Chapter 8

The High Road to Success

The crucible of success is composed of experience (knowledge), skill (learning what is productive) and utilizing one's strengths. After taking the financial personal profile from Humanagement we know our strengths and weaknesses. If we are intuitive, use your gut for all its worth. If low in analytical ability, don't postulate facts.

Profits come from seeing the momentum in a market early and taking the trade. The ability to monitor momentum helps not only stay with the trend but equally importantly to spot and trade trend reversals. Since many markets are related, if you spot a change in bonds, use it to trade stocks, commodities for interest rates, U.S. dollars for commodities, etc.

As important as being on the right trade at the right time is marking the profit when momentum is waning. The opposite of this is when we see weakness, go short and the market starts to rocket up. Take the small loss.

As childish as it seems, losses *really* bother, so when I get one I scream. I scream so loud the workers at the sawmill three miles away mistake it for the "go home" siren If this doesn't help make a trader more aware of losses and take appropriate action, nothing will. It also helps you to meet your neighbors.

Chapter 9

We Have Seen the Future, and it is Here

I started on Wall Street after graduating from the University of Washington in 1963. Don Delong, manager of Shearson, Hammill & Co. recruited me and I was off to 14 Wall Street. I had traded stocks and commodities during college and had a degree in Finance, but I had never been briefed on what being a registered representative of the N.Y.S.E. firm was about. I soon learned for many it was a party that led to a N.Y.S.E. test. We were taught compliance rules and regulations and how to pass a test and sell research ideas to the customers we found by cold calling, family friends and referrals. We were not taught how to make money in stocks and commodities for our clients. In 1963 brokers had quote machines, and research in 1993, to compete your research must be better than the brokers and so must your electronic equipment.

One of my clients on a give up basis was William O'Neill (Investors Business Daily). He would come in and trade what I considered the most volatile and, from my training the most risky of stocks. After all they had the most momentum, strongest charts (relative strength) and Shearson's research had no opinion on them. How could they be bought if we didn't recommend them? After all my manager thought these were "mumbo jumbo." I was the #1 producer in my class after one

13

year and had abandoned Shearson research and was deep into "mumbo jumbo." I later took O'Neill's course "How to Make Money In Stocks" three times—it indeed was deep mumbo jumbo and the more I got into it the more I liked it. My record has been good in large measure, I believe as a result of applying the rules I learned in the courses (my recent record: 1991 +155%, 1992 + 134%, 1993 + 66% to October 15).

In 1963 I attended Shearson's first Management Training Course. Upon completion I managed their main Los Angeles office. Charles Knapp was head of west coast corporate finance, an infamous victim of the S&L fraud of the 80's

I had several gurus along the way, including Bob Duggan, who influenced me to buy thin growth stocks and new issues the institutions would ultimately dump on the public. The magic of making money seemed to be able to read the tea leaves quicker, take the trades and head for the exit when the action stopped. Through the last 30 years I have been infatuated with mutual funds, hedge funds, institutional players, arbitragers, commodity traders and index computer driver programs. These were the good, bad and the very ugly. To be good you needed the edge.

Telecommunications and computer technology are largely responsible for the growth of the option and index markets. News is available much quicker and the emphasis on short-term performance compresses the movements and accents the movement (quicker and more efficient swings.)

It is now fairly simple for a bright investor with a reasonable amount of capital to make a substantial return on their capital. The hardware and software (including expert systems and neural networks is available at the drop of a hat), the trick is knowing how we naturally are composed and how we individually think. The trick is for the trader to marry himself or herself with the equipment and act out what the market communicates.

Markets are dynamic. They don't wait for us to get up to speed—they change, and good traders change with them (great traders have a high probability of anticipating and acting on trend changes). They can sell the over bought and buy the oversold markets.

I don't believe in being in the markets at all times; it also is a gut thing. It's like I was told to drive carefully and I'd reply "careful is my middle name." This is a system I'd recommend in addition to money management stops—sometimes after good or bad results just get out—the market tone does not feel right. Commissions should not be allowed to influence our decision to put on or take off a trade (they are small and meaningless). The decision should pivot around, would you buy it here? If not, get out! Sell it! Reverse it??

Chapter 10

Designing Personal Trading Systems

"Curve fitting" or selecting time and markets which give the best-optimized results is extensively used in selling trading systems. Those who design these systems for sale (you can look in technical trading magazines and see scores of them) are aware that parameter values (results) can be overfit to create results, I know. I traded a "stock box" S&P program for over a year with positive but mixed results. If one selected at random a market and a period, I'm sure the results would not be as staggering as what the designers show in their advertising.

What bugs me about a boxed system is that they pull it off the shelf without a clue as to whether it will meet your style (they do know the selected results meet your greed needs). Based on the Humanagement Test, had I taken it when I was training the system? I would know I'm high in intuition, not rules, discipline or analysis. I'm also not very mechanical, and I'm using a total mechanical system!

There are those who are great analysts. They can read Fed open market policy, they can read sentiment (contrarians at the tops and bottoms), puts and call open interest tells them public versus smart money and long term price momentum value line broad based index trend direction and support and resistance levels and utilize volume to see selling and buying presence. In addition, they have high IQ's in general, are steeped in earnings per share, balance sheet data, cash flow,

PE's relative to growth rates and all the items Wall Streets buy side wants. I would not rate their timing of their recommendations on a short term basis great since they usually are value oriented, not performance-results oriented. I.E., the guys telling you to buy XYZ are usually using fundamental data not meshed with technical or timing data. Those that use all three I think are especially valuable.

If we look back at your Humanagement Test results (if you did not take the test, go back and do so, or you are not getting your money—$—worth out of this book). The test will show your highs and lows (dominant/regressive) in:

1. Analytical ability
2. Intuitive makeup
3. Creative ability
4. Order—natural ability to follow rules

The four items above show why and how to overcome trading trauma and why our personal results aren't what they should be.

If you've ever had a bad ski fall and opted out from skiing the next day or for years, you know experientially what I mean. Trading trauma can be difficult to get over. The recovery involves learning what went wrong and taking measures to see the result is not repeated.

The mind burn needs to be resurrected and repaired. The bad experience needs to be turned into a learning experience. Recreate the losing event and learn what is needed to make the experience (result) different. Are you analytical, intuitive, creative/mixture or order oriented? Re-create the trade and input what was wrong based on your profile, then rehearse future trades until you feel good about your style. Some of this is a mix, i.e. are stop orders an affront to your analytical skills?

No matter what your trading profile makeup, stop loss protection should be a part of your routine to put you in a trade (higher or lower, lock in profits or limit losses). These mechanical stops are used to manage risk and trauma. If you are with me so far (stops are used to protect capital, profitable open trades and to prevent losses).then it is a basic requirement of stop order placement that one must admit that the markets can be right, and we may be wrong. Yes!!! While difficult to concede, stop losses promise you that tomorrow is another trading day.

For me, I lower trauma by using more stops. It increases profits and limits my loss.

Chapter 11

Your Style vs. "What Works"

There is no substitute in the market for knowledge and experience. The school of hard knocks amounts to a lot of study. Knowledge when compressed becomes form or style. Content/ideas are more important than form, but form cannot be neglected.

I used to trade like a "thirty pound weight on a two pound trigger." Now, when I trade "I work the order." This has become my style. This is not to say I don't trade "at the market." It is more accurate to state that I try to improve the market by trying to be high bid/low offer or trade in the middle of bid ask or utilizing selectnet or instanet. I can improve the net sales proceeds of my buy/sell orders by utilizing these services. If I shave a 1/16 or 1/8 nine times a week, my results are vastly different on an annual basis. My heavy trigger now has a velvet touch.

My style is also not to ever take any advise I don't agree with. Most of us don't want advice; we want to share our ideas with those who appreciate us. I refuse to do business with those I can't get along with or are too heavy handed with me. Life is too short. I recently closed an account with an experienced broker with a major firm because he was too pushy—I was not a fit for him and vice-versa. I take advice with a grain of salt—tentatively. To an apprentice in the market, advice from those knowledgeable is important. Ultimately we are our own best advisors.

1.   Evaluate your adviser.
2.   Understand the nature of the beast.
3.   Do your homework. Everything is somehow connected.
4.   Know what you want. Does your style achieve the results you want?
5.   You are the creator. You are in charge—the expert. Don't take advice you don't agree with! All you need is strong skills in money management, psychology and trading tactics.

You are the trader! You are wise, not because of what you know, but because of how you *understand* what you know. You are always at the center, at the core of your successful trading, and you always trade from that center. Your profits and enjoyment of trading sustains your endeavors. You perceive your involvement with the markets as a positive and powerful influence on your life—your daily trading leaves you energized, eager to return to your desk the next day because you are trading based o the volition of trading style influenced by your own personal intuition, rules, creativity and analysis. You trust trading yourself because you are utilizing your style. Do you like long term and short term trading, etc. It should not be a struggle to know how we think (what is natural for us) and trade that way. We don't need approval of others. Work with passion—you have found your niche in life (you are doing what you love to do and getting paid well for it.)

There is a reason I don't seek others advice: It is that in my experience there is a direct correlation between doing my own homework and results! If there is a positive between my effort and success, am I not better served and am I not more confident if I listen to what I learned than what someone else tells me? I have a healthy amount of skepticism, since a lot of advice on investments is "placed" by self-interested parties. Are they trying to create the other side of the trade?

I once knew Craig McFarland, a hedge fund operator (who is on his way to jail for defrauding banks). Craig called my next-door neighbor,

Larry Williams, and told him of a great stock that would soon double. I got a call from the market maker informing me that Craig had arranged to sell his stock to Larry—needless to say Larry had words with Craig and cancelled the trade with the market maker. Craig was creating the other side and this isn't usually done, so personally and the party "arranging" does not normally get caught! You should ask, what's in it for the sage advisor? What is their motivation?

Chapter 12

"Eldridge Axioms"

1. Nothing is funny when you're not making money.
2. Never make a bad position worse.
3. Never chase the market, let it chase you.
4. Hindsight is always 20/20.
5. When you don't know—do half.
6. Ask yourself—would you initiate at this price?
7. For every opinion—I'll give you another.
8. The market is not your friend—it takes no prisoners.
9. If the play is good—do it until your head caves in.
10. The moment you feel pressured to get out of your position is the moment I want the other side.

Chapter 13

Outlining Trades

Sometimes it helps unblock the essence of a trade by outlining the transaction.

1. Look at Chart (Higher Highs and Lower Lows). I like to buy strength and sell weakness. Trend player!
2. Fundamentals. What can I read and what is consensus forecast—will the company meet or beat its projections?
3. What time frame – day trade, several days, week, months? To me it is important to stick to the period selected. I monitor time and price. I have stops in mind regarding time and price.
4. Volume – does it increase or decrease on strength or weakness?
5. When I don't know what I'm doing, I panic. Outlining avoids chaos and panic. My outline is general and then specific, I break it into scenes so I know where I'm going. Carpe Diem!

My best trades unlock and are fluid because I've done my homework and am ready when the trade comes to me. I can hop on in its direction because I was waiting for it to take me aboard.

Homework can be fun if you keep to a daily schedule of chart review at a certain time for a limited period of time. If I don't do my work and a trade sets up or my brokers (I work with more than 30) call me and I don't know the trade, my experiential background persuades me to be internally a critic, since I was not prepared for the idea, I'm less open in the first place.

When I do my work I'm in full bloom and can say, YES!! I can do "size" because I know what is unraveling.

When I do my work I can be cunningly detached and aloof. I like to remain detached, as it is less stressful than attacking or forcing a trade. If you've done the research, collected data, reviewed charts, you are prepared mentally and emotionally. In your mental or narrative framework you already have the patience and concentration. There is no frustration, fatigue or resistance. You can hop on board in size and style. In short, the trader, investor is dramatically more prepared, spontaneous, and creative.

Chapter 14

Emotional Skills

Emotional skills, assuming you are not overriding your natural instinct, have all to do with yourself as an individual, not to do with the markets.

As you become successful trading stocks or futures, the process of learning begins and a combination of skills develops which are honed daily through volition in decisions. As you become a professional, leverage may come into play to increase percentage returns from the markets, this bringing into play emotional stress as the risk increases.

The opportunity to develop as an individual and realize monetary results is a powerful motivation. Concurrent with the motivation comes risk and emotional stress (nobody likes to lose!). The slings and arrows of the professional trader can produce serious emotional health problems. The way of healing stress is to understand yourself as well as having a keen understanding of trading strategy.

Trading is as much about finding methods by which to trade successfully as it is a journey inward. You must find comfort and confidence so you can "take" the stress of when the market offers its daily turbulence. It is a lot like fishing. It's not hard to get on board and buy a ticket for the ride. It's harder to see profits go to losses or losses go to profits. It's more difficult to sell than to buy. The emotional skill determines how much profit or how much loss. So, taking small losses are key and get to be "no big deal" – so is patience above all key and also "no big deal."

The reason I wrote this book is that after I tested with John Furey of Humanagement™, Inc., my trading and tremendous results – up 157% in 1991, up 134% in 1992 and up 60% in 1993 year through September – showed me I had found a method that fit the mold of my emotional and cognitive personality. My intuition is to never be on margin overnight, trade primarily OTC stocks, maybe 2/3 OTC and 1/3 listed, lots of new issues and secondaries and occasionally put out calls on indexes at overbought and oversold points using my own measurement of the markets. In 1994, I will begin trading futures with the same strategy with the inclusion of more overnight chart analysis, small considered positions, since I enjoy trading it will be fun and I'm confident profitable. The trick is to not get uptight and tied into knots and that is emotional skill.

The biggest lesson of all is small losses. Relating this to my experiences is my sophomore year of college. I took a job unloading boxcars of butter. I saved enough to buy 30 shares of American Photocopy at $22 for $660 plus commission. Within a year the stock was $6 and I sold it. Disappointed, disillusioned and discouraged! I refer to this as DDD.

Another DDD was the next summer when I worked for Peoples Bank of Seattle, now J.S. Bancorp Inc., I was doing income and financial statements for the trust department. That summer I saved up $500 and pooled it with $500 from my Dad in a joint a\c in commodities. We blew 80% of our capital in soybeans and pork bellies in two trades DDD!!! If I knew of small losses I might have made money in American Photocopy and commodity a/c. I owe a lot of gratitude to my father in letting me lose most of my money as it helped me learn small losses or DDD. My Dad didn't give up on me. On the contrary, he encouraged me to continue.

Continue I did. I had paper trades and more paper trades, which I traded seriously, and the losses were like life's blood. I didn't give up. I persevered and finished college with a degree in Business Administration, majoring in Finance at the University of Washington.

Like most champion athletes, champion investors must at some point have an inspiration dream or goal, which they steadfastly move toward.

Chapter 15

Intuition: Doing vs. Dreaming

I think we all know the vast difference between doing and dreaming. Yet, show me a winner who didn't make his dream reality by doing.

Creative people of whatever age or education have certain things in common. They challenge whatever is offered to them, even assumptions. They see in new ways; they visualize patterns, they connect and make networks. They take advantage of chance. Mistakes become "TAKES" to learn from. They go for it by taking risks.

Many schools of traditional thought stifle objective creativity. The current curriculum inspires obedience, not instinctive creativity. It strangles stimulation and inquiry. Creative development is stifled by the fear of being wrong – this is the prime inhibitor. Creative minds are sensitive. To them, joy is uncorked ecstasy, words have meaning, all thoughts connect, dreams become reality.

Chapter 16

Investing and the Internal Critic

In trading, particularly after a draw down (losing streak) the critics outside of us (family, clients, investment managers), those we fear we'll find in the audience, are a fundamental cause of blocking or failing to make a trade when one is available. But, they pale in comparison to an infinitely more threatening *voice* of censure, that of the critic within us. This is the most powerful and most common cause of investment blocking; the suppressive censorious voice of the internal critic.

The source of the critical voices is our own self. Why they are so powerful is that the internalized critic interrupts our creative pleasant thoughts with a dark, mostly clouded, thought. These clouds generally relate to the past bad losses or fear of future losses and interrupt our ability to be open to trades.

The internal critic is generally a protective figure who acts like a tyrant who is a perfectionist. The successful investor learns to cope with this inhibitive process with positive strokes about the present. This unlocks the block and frees us to trade.

Networking is very helpful whether it is your buddy, spouse, parent, child, or friend. It is good to talk to an objective party other than, but not excluding, your brokers. It really helps if I say "I've painted myself into a corner. Here is the fundamental technical reason. I (bought or sold) XYZ and it is up 7% or down 7%. It cannot help but increase the possible solutions. Then pick the one I like best. I cannot trade completely alone or completely reliant on others (it is the middle road, the one less traveled, that works for me). Decisions become less passionate, constructive, and self-confident because they are objective and a little less personal when we ask for the opinions of others.

Chapter 17

Backing the Trend

Those who buck the trend are called contrarians. Those who don't are lemmings. While I follow the trend and am a self-labeled lemming, I think one can do well either way – it depends on your grasp of the item in which you are invested. That is to say the perception of those who invest in the item after you. Either paying up or down and following the trend (long or short) or value investing implying buy low, sell high can consistently beat the market. To me, though, consistency means discipline or striking a single line of action. It involves having a plan (playing only fads – what's hot today or for the last three months) or, contrarily, not following the crowd and patiently being involved in less fashionable plays. Initial public offerings are a crowd following method of investing in what is popular and exciting at the moment. When human nature comes into play, fads can be put into orbit and ridiculous evaluations created. If you can take advantage of swings a lot of money can be made by being where the action is.

Value investing implies using a discipline in not getting carried away with what's hot at the moment and instead researching and investing in the unpopular and unfashionable.

Chapter 18

Matching Your Mind With Your Investments

The forecasting premise is that markets resonate which create circles of highs and lows (cycles) and these cycles can be traded profitably. Cycles vary in amplitude and can be varied by news (war and peace) and random events (political or weather related).

The mathematical premise of low risk and high rewards is simply to take history and computerize it and define profitability based on the relationship of X down days coming in to say a Friday followed by a gap down Monday and then buying above Friday's close. "Why?" you ask. Because if there is fear of war, election, economic problems which leads to a down week, this will be in the market by Monday and a turn about Friday will be profitable – you would not believe the high profitability of this simple trade over the years.

Market Philosophy –

A)   When trading take consistent size trades
C)   If in doubt, stay out
D)   More important than anything, predetermine the amount you are willing to lose before you take the trade! If down 5%, who cares, adios. Buy it back when the time is right.

E) To invest successfully one must first and foremost have a profound trust in oneself, and a sense of glorious possibility... One must visualize the results of using A.C.I.O. Analysis, Creative, Investigate, and Order.

F) There will generally and inevitably be a plethora of losses leading to a draw down. This excess losing period becomes a positive when the investors introspectively and humbly face their errors and separates the veils of traits which interweave to produce draw downs in their accounts. Losses generally produce a deep sense of exasperation, which can be used in a positive vein, if one recreates the fatal flaws which led to the losses in the first place. For example, did I over trade; not look at fundamentals, technical conditions of charts? Break any of the trading rules? Did I avoid analysis, intuition, etc.? This deep exasperation can be replaced with hope and positive "vibes" when one learns from the mistakes and moves back to one's plan, although the plan may be impacted and changed by the losses; then one can celebrate the unpredictable tenacity of grief associated with the losses, feel the loss, learn and MOVE ON to the tried and true or new plan.

In overhauling portfolios year after year, the familiar theme should be: Earnings Growth/Lack of Earnings Growth (Longs and Shorts).

Increased weighting can be made based on market bias (up or down) into stocks that post upward or downward momentum in earnings (long or short). As the sands shift one needs to keep close to the exit door both in growth (Microsoft 1993 High 98, Low 68, Last 71) and cyclical (Chrysler 1993 High 47 7/8, Low 18 7/8, Last 43). I don't spend a lot of time with low or High P-Es. It is like having a rocket with no fuel in the low P-E's or a jockey on a racehorse with no experience. It not only takes earnings growth but investors who are discovering that growth. Since markets are always emotional and earnings surprises or perception of that growth take stocks further on the upside and downside, it is important to have a disciplined plan which is objective, unemotional, and understanding of the nature of qualitative and quantitative market factors.

C   Create
I   Invest
O   Order
S   Seek

Volition is the use of your talent through conscious *choice* or self will. Volition is the foundation of one's instinctive will. Development of personal talent requires an assessment of our strengths and weaknesses and a desire to utilize this knowledge to increase productivity by quantifying our thoughts to improve our instinctive drive. To me, chaos can be order. Following my instinct is "going with the grain." Also, following instinct is less stressful.

One way of managing one's personal environment is to turn inward and suggest conceptually to the sub-conscious that you want to concentrate on improving your successful investment objectives. This unblocks you from the problem and lets your "Background Shadow Self" be eager and volitional in its pursuit or creative sub-conscious concentration.

I like to call this creative blockbusting. It asks the internal critic to give positive and negative feedback so one can generate a self-dialogue leading to positive decisions from a "friendly ear."

How you trade the markets and your style of approach can be a reflection of how you see yourself and your life. Your volition or choice in life may parallel your trading plan.

Slow – Analytical – Type B
Fast – Intuitive – Type A

Chapter 19

Systems Oriented

Who we are, how we think and our results are in great measure related to our experiences and what we have learned from them intuitively. Experience is the real teacher; life experiences, which you already have, can be reflected in trading plans. Trading profits come from willingness to surrender to a plan. One has to play and work with a plan until – It Comes Alive!

Until that mental connection between it and your uniqueness happens – until it surprises the hell out of you.

Talent is the species of Vigor and Volition.

Trust yourself, trust your experience, trust your feelings. Trust your intuition, your analysis, your rules and discipline, your absurdities. Trust your energy, involvement, commitment, momentum and passion. Passion provides aliveness and action. Trust it.

One secret of success in trading is to do that speculation on paper, not in your head. Over thinking results in paralysis by analysis. You wonder whether to pursue the trade, you rationalize – you can't decide so you do nothing. Analysis by definition is the separation of a whole into its parts for study. It is more harmonic as a whole before it is broken down and dissected. I can invest based on examination, but I can't trade that way. I need to check the idea and take the trade or pass.

Some frivolous-sounding, yet highly practical ways to simplify the choices are:

1.   "Eeny, meeny, miney, mo'" It works because it forces arbitrary decision – you don't care which outcome is best. It doesn't make any difference! Choose any one!

Another decision making process when you have two choices (i.e., trade/not trade). Simply flip a coin. Heads, one-way, tails the other. The secret is to match the emotional response to what comes up, and then follow that response, not the coin. The point is that the coin toss and your reaction to it have given you some information not in your conscious awareness. Try it!

Chapter 20

Jack Schwager

Prudential Securities Office, Wall Street, NY

Jack Schwager

Jack Schwager has been in futures since 1971 and is director of futures research for Prudential Securities, CEO of Wizard Trading, and author of Market Wizards, The New Market Wizards, *and* Schwager on Futures Series *(John Wiley & Sons'). To a great extent it is Jack who has brought to the public in published format the styles, disciplines and psyches of modern stock and futures traders. Jack started out as a fundamental analyst and in trading abandoned that methodology for the technical side. In this interview Jack explains what works for him and the secrets that have made him successful.*

LE: First off, let us address your general observations on traders and trading. Do you believe it would be possible to put together a team of traders where each member of the team would use their individual decision making methods to arrive at a common "team" trading decision?

JS: Conceptually, it could work. One of the trademarks of the good traders I've known and interviewed, however, is that they operate best as independent individuals. The best traders don't want to be confused by the opinions of others.

LE: Do you know of any "team trading" operations that have been successful?

JS: The only place I found where teamwork actually worked for trading is in firms such as Commodity Research Trading (CRT). CRT's operations resemble a manufacturing operation where everybody has his or her own task and individualism is downplayed. For example, they have people executing orders, other people generating the order sheets, research people developing strategies and computer mechanics to take care of computers when they go down. This type of operation, however, is not what people have in mind when they talk about trading.

LE: So you don't believe this is representative of trading or traders in general?

JS: Trading in the traditional sense is directional trading. CRT is actually an example of an arbitrage type of trading house. For this approach, a form of teamwork is probably the only way that will be successful.

LE: Then you believe traditional trading is more of a loner's game?

JS: Yes, I think that's absolutely true for discretionary traders, but not necessarily system traders.

LE: What about yourself?

JS: I used to believe that to be a successful trader, I had to operate totally solo. However, that was before I evolved to become a 100 percent systematic trader. Now, I consider my partnership with Louis Lukac, the other co principal of Wizard Trading, as an essential element in achieving success. I consider our partnership a prime example of teamwork working in trading.

We both share common philosophies about the market. We both believe in approaching markets totally mechanically and not emotionally. What makes our teamwork possible is that we work off each other's strengths. My strengths lie in the fact that I have many years of trading experience and my major weakness is a lack of computer skills. Louis' strengths are his extremely proficient computer skills and his weakness is his lack of trading experience. So, we meshed very well together by dividing the tasks. It's not as if we're working together and saying, "OK, here's the gold market, do you think it's going up?" That's not what we're doing. I'll write up a system idea I have and Louis will program it. Then we'll debug the system, make necessary modifications, evaluate whether and how to incorporate the system in our existing methodology the results, and discuss.

LE: Let's address trading methodology. How would you describe the methodology you and Louis use?

JS: First, it is one hundred percent mechanical in that we never deviate—even by a single contract—from the computer-generated trading signals. Second, the underlying assumption we have is that no single system can ever be derived that can always do well in every market. You can't capture the complexity of the markets with just a single system. So, we have developed a trading strategy based on a software structure that can take input from many different systems and mesh them together. In essence, what we've done is to find a way to combine lots of different strategies into one type of trading methodology and use computers to bring it all together.

LE: Do you use strictly a computer-evolved system or is your system augmented from what you may glean from looking at the charts and recognize as productive patterns?

JS: Everything always starts out as some idea I have—often chart inspired—which is then programmed into the computer. None of our systems are based on computer decision driven approaches, such as neural networks, where you give the computer a kitchen sink of variables and let it derive its own trading rules.

LE: Do you think computers enhance your trading skills?

JS: Well, it makes possible certain approaches that were impossible before. For example, twenty years ago, the approach we used would have required a computer larger than this room and a staff of technicians. Even then, the full program would have run slower than practical. So, our particular approach would have been virtually impossible many years ago. In that sense, the answer to your question is yes. Computers certainly make possible certain very complex approaches that would not have been feasible before.

LE: Do you think that computers seem to make the market less efficient or more efficient in terms of the movement that you've seen in the last couple of years?

JS: Efficiency is really a function of liquidity. Insofar as computers have made possible a dramatic expansion in trading volume, they have made the markets more efficient.

LE: How do you feel about currently available computerized trading systems?

JS: I can't say since I am not familiar with systems sold to the public. I do know, however, that if you would come in with a check for five million dollars for our methodology, I wouldn't sell it to you. So, I have to question why people out there are selling computer-trading applications for anywhere from $300 to $3,000. I'm very skeptical why anyone with a novel and extremely productive approach would sell it.

JS: And, by the way, our results don't even come close to those promised by the trading system ads. Kind of makes you wonder.

LE: Have you ever purchased and used any over-the-counter computer applications for your trading?

JS: I don't buy systems. I've always realized that I'd have trouble following somebody else's trading decision rules.

LE: Of the software trading packages that are available for people to buy, which are most useful?

JS: There's no answer to that, because it depends on the person. I am basically a user of different types of charts; weekly charts, monthly charts, daily charts, and intraday charts. That's it. I don't use oscillators or other indicators. Moving averages are okay, but I don't use other than as one of the hundreds of inputs in our computerized trading approach.

LE: How do you enter and exit trades?

JS: I don't think of our approach on a trade-per-trade basis. A better description would be to say that our methodology adjusts the position size in each market, each day. For example, if today's position weight in the Japanese yen is + 60% and yesterday's position weight was +56%; we would buy 4 percent of a full position today.

LE: So, your system doesn't change until after the close each day?

JS: That's right. It's run every day after the close.

LE: Would it be a refinement to have it work during the day before the market closes?

JS: We have an agenda of more important tasks. We have a list of projects and far down that list is intraday trading strategies. The reason it's low on the list of priorities is because there is an exponential increase in terms of work and a questionable payoff at the end.

LE: Is pattern recognition part of your methodology?

JS: As I said, our approach combines different strategies. One segment of those strategies might come under the label of pattern recognition.

LE: When you say pattern recognition, what do you mean?

JS: Pattern recognition is anything that relates to types of price combinations. It could be something very simple. For example, in one set of systems that we employ, we look at what I call "wide ranging days." Wide-ranging days are days where the range, the spread between the high and low, is significantly larger than the average range of the recent period.

That's an example of a very simple one-day pattern. You could define larger patterns or combinations of patterns. Sometimes it's hard to draw a line between what is pattern recognition and what are conventional trends. The lines get blurred.

We make the following distinction between trend and pattern systems. Trend systems, by definition, will always catch every major trending market. They can't help but catch the trend. The downside is that trend-following systems will enter trades late and exit trades late. They will also get chopped to pieces in sideways markets. A pattern recognition system, however, seeks to identify patterns associated with trend transitions, and will, hopefully, be quicker in getting in the right market direction than would a conventional trend approach. The tradeoff is that the pattern recognition system may miss a trend altogether, because the pattern you're looking for may not set up.

For example, assume we had an approach where you would go long when the market close is higher than the high of the most recent wide-ranging day. That is a pattern recognition system. It may sometimes get you long near the bottom and short near the top, but it may also fail to provide any timely signal in a major trend.

LE: What do you think of straight pattern recognition? For example, assume you noticed that a down Thursday and a down Friday were followed by an up Monday 60% of the time.

Looking at the historical record, you decide you will buy on any Monday following back-to-back declines on Thursday and Friday. Would that be a valid methodology?

JS: That type of pattern of recognition is very prone to error because if you take any samples of data, you will always find some combination of buying on certain days and selling on other days, that could have been profitable *in the past.* If you look at enough combinations, you can't help getting some very good results. It is like flipping ten coins over and over again. Theoretically you should get ten heads about once every thousand trials.

LE: What oscillators do you use or find valuable?

JS: I'm not an oscillator fan so I really don't use any oscillators at all, other than in a contrary way. In other words, when I use oscillators, I'm using them in a way that is opposite the way most people use them.

LE: In other words, you don't believe in using oscillators as overbought or oversold signals.

JS: I haven't expended enormous research on the subject, but I have satisfied myself that reasonably simple, straightforward applications of oscillator strategies do not work. Any oscillator-based system we have tested, where oscillators are interpreted as overbought/oversold indicators, have been substantially inferior to a wide variety of other systems we have developed. I am sure there are traders who have found useful ways of applying oscillators, but I don't think there's anything very special there, and I think that the way most people use oscillators generally does more harm than good.

LE: In your role as research director for Prudential Securities are your recommendations also computer-based?

JS: No Louis and I have designed some computerized systems that generate daily signals, but my day-to-day recommendations as an analyst are chart-based.

LE: When you look at your charts, are you trying basically to find up trends and downtrends, or do you look for other things?

JS: I am looking for patterns and combinations of patterns. For example, let's say I see a pattern developing that in my experience is usually followed by a downtrend, I will be inclined to trade the short side, regardless of whether the trend is up or down – although I am less likely to go against the trend.

LE: Do you use objectives on your recommendations?

JS: When I'm putting on a trade, I don't prejudge where I'm going to get out, other than to say where I'll get out if I am wrong. If a move has lasted for a while, both in terms of magnitude and duration, I may sometimes consider exiting on an objective.

LE: Now let's talk about your trading as a CTA. Do you alter your position size depending on the market?

JS: Of course, we will adjust position size to the volatility of the market. That is, all else being equal, we will trade more contracts in the less volatile markets. But a more subtle distinction is that we will vary our position size within each market, which is an important element in our trading approach. Our methodology by its very nature will tend to vary position size. The net position will depend on the balance of many different inputs. So, our position size will vary a great deal depending on certain conditions.

LE: What do you mean by conditions?

JS: By conditions, I mean the net impact of all the strategies that have been programmed. In other words, if a great preponderance of those strategies are all pointing in one direction, we will have a much heavier position than if there is a near balance between bullish and bearish signals.

LE: How do you deal with losing trades?

JS: One of the points I have tried to make in my books, and which I believe in more and more, is that winning traders don't agonize about losing trades because they realize losing is just part of the process of winning. Nobody can sit down and win at every trade. You are going to have losses, no matter how good you are. Winners aren't bothered by losses because they believe that they will keep winning in the long run. It's just like a hiker traversing a series of rising hills, who knows he can't go from one peak to the next without going down in between. When winning traders go down, they have the knowledge and confidence that they will go up again. Losses mostly impact and hurt those people who don't have that confidence.

LE: What percentage of your equity do you lose on a bad trade?

JS: We don't think in terms of individual trades or track our trades that way. In our approach, we determine the theoretical position each day and adjust our position size accordingly. For example, if in a $1 million account we are long seven gold contracts at the end of the week and our computer run for Monday indicates that our position size should be eight; we would buy one gold contract on Monday. If the next day's run shows we should be long six gold contracts, we would then sell two gold on Tuesday. Now is one of the two contracts we sell on Tuesday the one we added on Monday, or are they both trades implemented earlier? Frankly, we don't even bother to define it, because we don't care about individual trades.

LE: How do you control risk if you don't monitor individual trades?

JS: We try to limit the risk several ways. First of all, we're very diversified. We trade as many markets as we can. Our primary portfolio trades 60 markets. Second, we use so many different strategies that we rarely take a full position in any market because they're contradicting each other. Third, we employ a money management strategy that dynamically adjusts our trading size in every market and the overall portfolio in line with changing market volatilities. In other words, we always keep our theoretical risk constant regardless of what the markets are doing. Fourth, we also use other proprietary money management strategies that I don't care to detail.

LE: Do you change stops daily in your managed accounts?

JS: Stops introduce a vulnerability to sharply increased slippage, particularly for large size orders. We achieve risk control through other means.

LE: Jack, in comparing your findings regarding various traders, do you see a parallel between how people think and how adaptive they are and does that combine or contribute to their becoming successful traders?

JS: I believe that successful traders gravitate to an approach that matches their personality. In my opinion, Paul Tudor Jones is an example of one type of extreme. He operates by seeming to have the ability to gather information from several sources simultaneously. For example, while watching several monitor screens in his office, he takes telephone calls, shouts out orders, and talks over his loudspeaker. If you know Paul, you would expect him to be that way because he has that type of personality.

LE: Then someone like Paul Tudor Jones could thrive in chaos and be perfectly all right?

JS: It appears to me that to someone who operates like Paul, it is not chaos. These types of people seem to have the ability to take in information simultaneously from several different sources and then mesh it all together and come to a decision with some sort of intuition.

LE: Do you know anyone that would be an example of another type of extreme?

JS: Gil Blake. His personality and methodical trading style to my mind the exact polar opposite of Paul Jones. Gil has rules that are geared to make just one trade decision a day. Gil is a fund timer and his approach is to look for patterns in funds. He is very soft-spoken and has a very low key, very unassuming type of personality. His style of information gathering and decision-making involves going to the library and getting reams of price sheets from the microfiche. He then goes through them and looks for patterns almost like an accountant. It seems his trading style and personality are closely related.

LE: If it were determined that a person had a high degree if intuition, how much credence would you advise that person to put into intuition versus mechanical evaluations?

JS: If you have extremely good intuitive skills, I believe it is possible to work off that as opposed to using a more systematic or analytical approach. But you still need some sort of money management plan to survive.

LE: What advice would you give to people wanting to be successful traders?

JS: Don't worry about filling out the areas that you're weak in. Find out where your strengths lie, and just concentrate on what you're strong at and forget about the rest. I think that success lies in knowing and using your strengths.

LE: Thank you for your time, Jack.

JS: You're welcome!

Chapter 21

Skip Raschke

Skip graduated from Gonzaga University in 1971 and was dually drafted by the U.S. Marines and the New York Yankees, where he pitched for 3 years. In 1974 he got registered as a broker with Mitchem, Jones and Templeton (now Paine Webber). Skip worked on the Pacific Coast Stock Exchange trading options and stock, where he met his wife Linda Bradford and has traded options and stocks on the Philadelphia Stock Exchange since 1982.

SR: Over the last series of stocks like Waste Management, MCA, Campbell Redlake which became Placer Dome, and Martin Marrietta, a pretty big aerospace company. Most recently, in the last year, I've moved from the options side of the exchange to the equity side where I'm a specialist with a company called Hurricane Trading. It's one of the larger privately owned firms on the exchange. We're involved not only in equity options, but also currency options which is very big on the Philadelphia exchange, and of course the equity side which is where I'm a specialist for the firm. I'm a specialist in thirty-four stocks that are New York Stock Exchange stocks that are duly listed, in other words, on our floor. We also are one of two firms that are involved in a pilot program with the NASDAC in that we make markets in a series of stocks: in particular, US Health Care and Sun Microsystems, to name a couple of them. There are ten of them total but those are just two that pretty much demand most of my time when it comes to making markets that really count. So I'm quite busy. I have business coming in either from listed stocks, from people who are either buying and/or selling, and of course I'll be on the other side or I've got business to take care of relative to making markets over the counter and we also do agency business for traders in the over the counter market where sometimes I will take the other side of their trade, other times I'll strictly go to whoever is bidding or offering the other side with what the trader wants to do and let it go through me as an agent. I have quite a lot of decisions to make during the day.

LE: So you are laying off your risk, you take a trade on much like a trader in options: they're not sure which way the stock's going so in order to move their inventory they lock up a hedge long stock/short stock or protected with puts or calls as the case calls for.

SR: Right, Right. What we're trying to do every day of course is to go home as flat as possible or when it comes to equity positions where we use options to hedge, we want to go home as close to neutral as possible. That's using of course the measurement of options being dealt us so we're always looking to come off the floor every day as close to neutral as possible. I particularly like to play from what's known as the positive gamma side of the options market where if a stocks going to move one way or another I'm moving with it, I'm willing to pay the premium in order to do that but I wanna always be with the trend of the stock. In other words, I'm not crazy about stepping up to the plate and buying something that's getting hammered or selling something that's rising pretty rapidly. I would like to have a position where I get longer going up or I get shorter going down. Thus if I buy a stock, I'll generally buy, for each share of stock, I'll buy a couple of puts equivalent to that, which give me two different opportunities here. One, should the buy of the stock not be a good buy, initially, the additional put allows me to average my price by buying again at a better time at a better level, or, of course, if it does take off then I strictly have to have a move in the stock that pays for the put premium that I paid in the first place in order to protect myself. I'm just very leery of taking an equity position without owning puts underneath. I think of puts as being stops. I know if I buy XYZ at thirty and I buy the thirty strike put, I know that, based on the premium I paid for the put, I know that I'm going to be stopped out by that particular put. My risk is locked.

The same is true on the shorting side. If I'm shorting stock, I want to be the long call. I don't strictly like to short something and not have upside protection, and once again, buying calls is similar to buying puts with long stock, buying calls against short stock is the prudent way to play.

One thing I do see in the market today from being an equity specialist that was a little bit surprising when I first encountered it is that what I am doing is pretty unusual and rare. I don't see too many other specialists hedging themselves, which gives me a little pause for concern, only because after seeing what's happened in the last 20 years in the market, which isn't all that much, when you consider that markets go back hundreds of years in history, but the last 20 have been just incredible when it comes to historical volatility. I just don't understand how you can walk off the floor every day in a short condition or a very long condition without it being hedged. I just couldn't sleep, and of course the old maxim of trading down to your sleeping point, maybe these guys have stronger sleeping points than I do, or deeper wallets, I guess. It's just, to me, the modern way to trade, and it's always going to be this way, and I think that I'm a little in the forefront of that game. But I just like to be in a hedged position. I don't like to be unhedged.

> LE: Would you like to maybe give a little of your philosophy in terms of where we've been and where the market is going?

> SR: Sure, no problem.

Since the crash of '87 and the mini-crash of '89 – they were crashes, no matter what Wall Street revisionists try to tell you, they were crashes. There was complete panic, total chaos, and total loss of control across the board from institutional to specialists, you name it, certainly the public. It's my best guesstimate that we have learned nothing from the crash of '87. All we've done is we've kind of put a finger in the dike, with these collars or whatever. I think that Victor Hugo said it, that no one can stop an idea when its time has come. No one could stop '87 and nobody is going to be able to stop the next one. The wipeouts come when you least expect it when markets are looking like there's no downside problem at all, and everything's rosy and, out of nowhere, something hits, and it starts the snowball going downhill. What's going to happen this time around, as best as I can see it, and when it happens is the big timing question, and it's not a matter of if, it's when, so if you plan as I am, you're constantly looking over your shoulder to see if the Indians are getting near.

There are a lot of elements you've got to look at. There's certainly the public attitude. Public attitude is getting more and more bullish. The institutional money is constantly growing, it seems, and in that particular case, we're talking mutual funds and money managers. The mutual fund industry, since '85, I think has at least doubled, if not tripled. We had somewhere around 1500 mutual funds in '85 and I think we have 4000 now. We have more mutual funds than we have stocks on the New York Stock Exchange and the American Stock Exchange combined. When you look at a Wall Street Journal, there are more mutual funds on the pages than stocks in the two exchanges. It's crazy. Of course, you had a pretty good market to draw in that kind of money, but it seems to me like each day an analyst, or whoever is pulling the trigger at these funds, has got to come up with a new reason to buy. They're constantly, in my mind, fooling themselves into thinking buy buy buy. They're not being cyclical in their thinking. They're being linear. They're drawing straight lines. The straight line thinkers were the guys back in the 80s who saw oil go from 4 to 8 to 16 to 32, and next thing they took out their rulers and they had it going to a hundred. In fact, I think that one of the administrative biggies predicted a hundred dollar barrel of oil within a few years. And of course, that was right around the top. I think it peaked out around 35 or 40. But, what I'm getting at is that is linear thinking. That's straight line thinking, taking out a ruler and drawing a straight line to the moon. That's not the way the market works. It can go for quite awhile in the same direction, but sooner or later, the cycle eventually starts to come into play, and then you go through the stages that I know exist within the cycle.

There are four stages. The bottom of the cycle is despair. You come out of despair going up the optimistic leg. At the top is euphoria. That's where the whole world loves it. No one sees the potential for decline. And coming out of euphoria is hope. If you draw a sine wave, which is essentially an S on its side, and label the stages 1, 2, 3 and 4, one being the bottom (despair), two going up to optimism, three the top (euphoria) and four coming off the top (hope), and ask me to gauge where we're at right now, in this particular market I'd say that we're near the peak of euphoria. We're seeing quite a few of the silly things that you do see at the top, and, as far as how long it can take, euphoria can last quite awhile. In terms of this market, in points, I think it could last for a while longer. We're at a little over 3600 today; it wouldn't surprise me to see 4000 on the Dow. I've seen a few people who have already started to push that number. Why that's a big number, I don't know, but as bearish as I can be, I thought 3700 was going to be about it, and this was two years ago. To me, that's my number. If it can get into that range, I'll probably start looking into selling the market and maybe buying a few more calls on top of it in case it does want to get crazy, because what we can do in a market that we're in right now is have a blowoff.

Bull markets, in the past, have ended in blowoffs. It wouldn't surprise me if this one would, either. A blowoff where the shorts capitulate and all this hot money that wants to come into the market, but has been afraid and wants to make sure that what they do with the money is the right thing to do, which, of course, is buying at the top. That could all come together as one cataclysmic blowoff to the upside, which could be triggered by anything, I don't know, like somebody cutting the prime, or something goofy. But that, to me, would be the signal, in which case I would want to own a few more calls at around a 3700 level. Then I'm short stock only as a hedge because of that last surge potential, because I would definitely want to reshort the market in and around the 3900 to 4000 range which, while I keep talking those incredible numbers and we're talking about some incredible historical events happening in that case like Dow Jones going to record highs, PEs record highs. You know, we laughed back in the 80s at the Japanese for having stocks that were trading at 50 to 70 times earnings. Today, I see them all over the place, from the over the counter market even down to the New York Stock Exchange stocks and people are justifying the purchase of these stocks, whereas in many cases they are the same people who were laughing at the Japanese PEs back in the mid 80s before they crashed. And, if you look at what happened to the Japanese, that should be your warning. I mean, we went to what, 38000 on their Dow and dropped down to around 15000 in six to eight years after their peak was hit. To think that we're not going to do the same thing, or somewhere close to it, I think, is not using the history the way the way it ought to be used. You should visualize the potential for a serious selloff before it starts.

If I could draw my perfect world, I'd like to be long on the blowoff, when the thing ends, no matter where the number is, where it ends, 3700, 4000, I don't care. I'd like to catch that blowoff and I'd want to definitely be shorting into that and hang onto your hats coming down, because what I think you're gonna see is a blood bath in the mutual funds industry. Keep in mind going back to '85 when you had those 1500 mutual funds, now you've got 4000, which means you have about 2500 people managing these funds, since that particular time who haven't managed funds before. They haven't seen what I consider to be a decent bear market. A decent bear market to me, you've gotta go back to the '70s when we had those kind of things, it's almost like they've been outlawed for the '90s, they can happen and if you look at what happened to mutual funds from the close of 1972, of mutual fund XYZ, let's call it $100 per share, at the end of '73 and '74, that $100 was somewhere around the $44-$45 per share level after that two-year bear market. You put that into today's numbers, let's say the Dow does get to 4000, you're talking basically a Dow under 2000 at the end of a two-year bear market. This is equivalent to what could happen. Given the state of affairs we've got today in the mutual fund industry, should that similar historical parallel take place, and that would be a twenty year cycle, which there's enough of them around.

Let's go back to '87. What you had in '87, you had the crash. You had the ability at that point to sell your stock, to swing over to the bond market with some of your money and to this point, today, you'd probably get all of your money back. What you lost in equity in '87 if you went long bonds at that particular point, getting out of the market around Dow 2000, taking that money and swinging into bonds, you probably got all of your money back if not some more if you held from that point to today.

The big difference between that point and now is, not only is the stock market reaching its apex, the bond market has already done it, or is darned close to it. You know, bonds used to be around 120 whatever, I guess they could get to 123 or 125, at a yield of somewhere around 5½ on the long bonds, something like that. I mean, once again, anything could happen when things get crazy and human emotions and euphoria set in. Euphoria, by the way, is described in the dictionary, among other things, as a false sense of well being, so, there's your caveat. The difference now is that you can't sell stock at a decent price on a selloff when you realize you're trending down and you think, "Oh, God, I've better sell my stock. I think I'll take that money and go into the bond market. If you do that today, not only are you going to get ripped in the loss in your stock, but by the time you buy bonds, you're probably buying at the top of that market, too. So, why would that be? Probably because when the next bear market begins, it's going to begin in and around the time that interest rates are going to start rising. It would be heaven for the shorts and hell for the longs, and it's probably the next major cycle that's setting up. I don't see what's going to stop it. It's just a matter of seeing it coming and taking advantage of it. Yeah, the scenario that could easily contribute to all of that would be the economy has to turn the corner, but we're going to stagflate similar to the mid 1970s to early 80s. Inflation will start coming back because the economy is turning up. Money will start getting a little tighter, certainly the Feds and the Hawks will take over there, and they will start moving up rates and when everybody turns to look to see who they can sell their stocks or bonds to, there won't be anybody left because, pretty much everybody's wallets are going to be empty, having gotten caught in euphoria. We see it all the time, throughout history, you saw it in the real estate market in the early '90s after the big blowoff in the '80s. Nothing's going to stop it from happening in the stock and bond market because that's the nature of things, they cycle. Once again, we're going to have to teach a whole new crop of people that that is the way of the financial world. Things don't go straight up or straight down, but we've been going up for quite a long while with both the stock and bond markets straight up. But all we've been in is just a cyclical market that will give way to a cyclical bear market. The mutual fund industry is not prepared for this. They've had tremendous growth and there's going to be one hell of a weeding out process when it hits. The mutual fund industry doesn't short stock; almost all of us don't hedge. The few that do hedge will probably be the ones who do OK, or at least don't get annihilated, but I'd say that 90+ percent of them don't hedge, in which case they're gonna be long gone.

The Investment Company Act of 1940 allows for some neat things to take place. Regarding mutual funds, and what mutual fund managers can do, they're pretty much obscure, unknown rules or escape clauses for these people. If I'm correct on this, they're gonna become quite well known, even when it all hits, when you know what hits the fan. Two points that I'm trying to make are:

1) A mutual fund's manager doesn't have to redeem your shares for seven business days if he feels that he is in a very unusual period in the market. I think that has been defined as everybody wants to sell and nobody wants to buy and if I hit a bid here, I'll only be making things even worse and I really can't find a buyer anyway for what I'm trying to sell, so I'll just hold off for a few days until everybody comes to their senses. He's allowed to do that per the Investment Company Act of 1940. I think it's in some of the prospectuses. I have seen some

prospectuses for mutual funds where it's not even mentioned in there, but I've also seen somewhere it is. I don't know off of the top of my head which ones do and which ones don't, but, as I said, if this all comes to pass we're gonna see it because there's gonna be a situation where these fund managers are going to hold off redeeming your shares. So, let's say that you're dealing with XYZ funds. You see the market begin to sell off, it's down 200 points, you're getting a little concerned, and all that, and you call up and you say sell all my funds, I have 5000 shares with you guys and I want them all sold. You look at the next morning and you see that, even though it's gone from $22.00 down to $20.50, you know you called that fund and told them to sell you out, and that's the price you're expecting to get. Well, lo and behold, they haven't really sold off your shares because the funds manager has decided that he is going to withhold redemptions due to some unusual market situation. Now, you can see the danger here as it starts to build. If enough of those guys think the same thing, and they're all waiting for Chicken Little to quit screaming that the sky's falling, but yet the sky really is falling, then you have a potential for a panic, and you're gonna have one hell of a batch of unhappy customers that aren't gonna be happy that you didn't sell them out when they told you to. The customers think they are guaranteed that 20.50 dollar price, and the manager's gonna wait that 2, 3, 4 or maybe that full 7 days that he's allowed to go through before he finally does redeem. Well let's say that all takes place and by the time the redemption notice comes through the mail he got you out at 17. You aren't going to be too happy. And I think this is going to happen because there's too much of an opportunity for these guys to take advantage of this. I think I saw some of this throughout the crash period in 1987. What you had back then was, you had Cassandras running around. You had people saying "Look out, the sky is falling." and they were right. They were early, but they were right. Guys like Precter and some of the other popular names. At least they got the press. They got your attention and that kept enough money on the sidelines, I think, to start the turnaround in the market, even though it took about two months for that market to really bottom out, I think December was really the bottom in 87, when all stocks had made their bottom by then. So, back then, you had those Cassandras, today you don't. Which means that we really don't have anybody passing on the message that you shouldn't be putting all your money to work into this particular market at this particular level. It's pretty dangerous. So, you're building up a situation where, if all this does come to pass, you're gonna have a whole lot of people wanting to sell, and the old battlecry's gonna be, Ok, sell, fine, but to whom? I want to make the other point about the mutual fund industry in that, should they get to a situation like that, and they've got an obscure company Digital Datawhack or something and they've gotta couple million shares in the portfolio and they're marking it on a daily basis of, let's say, $10 per share, but the biggest bid they've got is $2 a share because it's basically an illiquid stock that they never thought would become illiquid or they never thought that the market would just go to pot like that on them, what they can do is, they can mail you your percentage of the shares that you own based on how many shares you own in the fund. Now, that's going to make for an interesting situation, too, because here you are ....

[Break in tape.]

What's gonna happen is that Mr. Jones is gonna get in the mail this Digital Datawhack, like 200 shares or 500 shares, or whatever, mailed to him from XYZ fund with a letter saying, gee, we tried to find a buyer and couldn't. So, here, it's yours, you get rid of it. It'll be, of course, written up a lot prettier than I just stated it, but when you cut through all the BS, that's how it's really gonna read. And that's going to destroy the confidence of all those customers within that fund and if it's going to happen in one fund, you know it's going to happen in another fund, and it's going to ripple throughout the industry to where these people who are running these funds are gonna have to come up with a good line in order to keep their customer base up. They won't be able to. I think there will be such a negative attitude on the part of the public when they see that they are losing money all over the place that it's just gonna continue the downward pressure on the market. It's something that's not gonna be overcome within weeks.

One thing that we've seen that's built up since '87 and has been especially reinforced since '89 is what I call the buy dippers. These people have been buying dips since '87 and '89 and have been winners, and, you know, bless them, I think that's great, and I'm glad that they could do it. On the other hand, to constantly do something over and over again without mentally gearshifting or being prepared to mentally gearshift is extremely dangerous when it comes to trading stocks or bonds or options or anything. Once again, that's using linear thinking, straight line thinking that I'm always going to get away with buying a dip. What's probably gonna happen in the next bear market that takes place is that those people are going to get wiped out because they've been doing the same thing over and over again and they're going to buy a dip and they're going to realize this ain't just a dip, this thing is going down a long flight of stairs and all they've done is that they've bought the leveling off of the first down leg and that next down leg will probably be even more vicious than the first and they've already bought the dip once, what are they gonna do the second time? Well, if they've got more money, more than likely human nature says "No, I'm not wrong, I'm right, I'm just getting a chance to buy another dip". They'll buy into that next flight of stairs down. Same thing, it'll level off, and I think that this will just continue until you finally have destroyed enough of these people who have been buying dips and their fund manager's will be just a guy on the street who doesn't make any difference. There's the biggest pool we've ever created of them out there and they're going to give the shorts an opportunity to make a heck of a lot of money because if you caught that particular crowd at the right point, and more than likely they'll be wrong, then you can't help but make a lot of money on the short side. The situation is right for it. It's just a matter of timing now, and the timing shouldn't be all that far away. I'd say somewhere within, I'd say no longer than six months, and it might have already started, for all I know. Point is, that if you're going to be involved in the stock market, you've got to think cyclically. If you're going to keep doing the same thing over and over again, it's like saying the same thing over and over again, like saying the sun's going to rise, well here you're right, but at dusk it's going down. But if you want to keep saying the sun's going to rise, you're right, it's just a matter of how long you can continue to do that with the stock market until we go into a pretty long winter. I think that's not too far away. Actually, in a sick way, I'm kind of looking forward to it. Oh, I've always been a bear because I love to sell them first and buy them back later. It's kind of like running a store. As a market maker steps on the floor, he has no inventory. How do you create inventory? People want to buy. Well, you've got to sell, and you've got to sell what you don't own. It's called selling short. Actually, someone told me a long time ago the first short sales was described in the old testament: someone sold a crop that he hadn't even planted yet, so it's not like I invented it. It goes back a few thousand years.

The market maker mentality on the options floor is what is in the back of my thinking and any particular stock that I've traded I enjoyed trading on the short side only because the public is the other side of the market maker's trade and the public doesn't normally short. The public buys. When the public does start shorting, that's when you know the turn is pretty close and you can start moving to the long side of the market. I've also found, too, that it's the most rewarding and it's the quickest reward you can receive in the market. We climb stairs one at a time, but we slip on a banana peel and we wind up at the bottom a whole lot faster than it took going up those stairs, and that's just the way the market works. So, I like waiting for those banana peels to be placed on those steps and basically don't mind if someone slips on them, because that's where the big money comes and comes fast. So, yeah, I do take the bearish side only because that's the most rewarding. It's also the one that allows me to be a contrarian. I hate being on the side of the majority, I know the minority makes money in the market, not the majority and that's another thing I don't like is too much company. I know generally that shorting anything, you don't have that much company. There's a paradox there because it sounds like you're fighting the tape in a sort of way. But, you're really not. What you're doing is timing your entry on the sell side and waiting for the buyers to exhaust themselves, because once they do the market tends to correct itself quite quickly. So, yeah, I do enjoy the short side only because of its rewards. I don't enjoy seeing all the cataclysm in the market when the bad news hits because I know a lot of people are getting hurt. It has nothing to do with that. In fact, I was on the trading floor in the crash of '87, and I did quite well. I was long hundreds and hundreds of puts on different stocks that just made tons of money. But it was the strangest thing. I had this sick feeling in my stomach and a sad feeling because I saw friends of mine getting hurt. It's kind of like you're in a fox hole and the enemy's attacking. I was in the marine corps, so I'll throw that analogy out. You haven't been shot, but you see your buddies in other fox holes that have been hit pretty hard and you don't feel elated by something like that even though you know you're gonna get out of there ok. You feel pretty sad about it. I don't want to see it happen. I hope to hell that I'm wrong. I hope the Dow goes to 10,000. I mean, that's fine with me all the way. On the other hand, there's nothing wrong with making money, and I know the quickest way to make money is to wait for the bears to take over.

I'll always hedge even though I might short IBM at 50, I'll still own a couple of 50 stock calls just in case I'm wrong. I'll always hedge, but what I think I'll see coming, and I try to envision these scenarios so that if and when everything does line up and does start to happen, I'm totally prepared. Going back to '87 once again, I thought the market was going to go down starting in August of '87, I thought it had a six month window to go down and I told my father-in-law, you mark my word that this market is going down 200 points one day. I remember that he laughed at me, and I said "No, I'm dead serious. I think the Dow has the chance to drop 200 points in a day. Well, we didn't drop 200 points in one day, we dropped 500 in one day. The thing is, that I was prepared for something that nobody had ever seen before only because I saw the potential for it. So, what I'm doing everyday is thinking about what is going to cause this bear market to get rolling and create this out of hand scenario that I can see. Definitely the interest rates are going up, definitely the economy is turning up or at least coming to grips with the fact that the economy is strong enough to warrant higher interest rates environment, meaning that money is going to become tighter and inflation should start to pick up and an excessive amount of bullishness on the part of the public, low cash in the hands of the institutions, and generally a feeling that nothing can go wrong and everything looks rosy. Or the other situation that we mentioned before was a blowoff on the upside, a ridiculous day, what was the ridiculous amount that we snapped back after the crash, say we're up 200 in a day on the Dow. That would definitely raise my shorts, my short horns to the roof. I'd be all over them to move on the sell side. So, it can become emotionally, technically or fundamentally. If all three happen to come at once, the more bearish I will get. That's a day to day thing, hour to hour, actually. To see that out there is one thing, to be prepared for it is another. What I am right now, is just prepared, that's all.

LE: The Stalking Bear!

SR: I know the enemy's out there and I'm just waiting for him. What will start it is when I first spot a lagging advance decline line, lower volume rallies, stocks rolling over, bike it. Those are the things I'm looking for to spot it.

LE: Well, you know, I think we've come a long way in terms of discussing historically where the market has come from, and discussed past and future mini or major crashes and it's interesting in this time period of so many bulls, so much money going into stocks, so much money going into bonds, here is someone to take a contrary opinion and basically take the position of being prepared for it. I'm sure that people who are throwing their money into mutual funds aren't thinking of anything but a rosy future. Here we are in the middle of October of '93 and it will be interesting to come back a year and a half from now and see where we've gone.

SR: Definitely. I want to mention one other point, too, that the market history is full of downward pockets that have hit markets that are in circular full trend. So, it's not unusual to have something go wrong along this yellow brick road that we're on. If you go back and read the history of the markets from the 1870s to the early 1900s, and you put that on a parallel to today as to what could happen, those markets were ripe with what we would call today bear markets. I don't care what you call them. Stocks were basically $60 one day and $40 the next. I know we talked earlier about this company Synergen that changed people's perception on the options floor as to what can happen. That's something that I've been preaching to my friends, if they'd just listen. That was the shot across the bow. Stock trading in the mid 40s opened up in the mid teens from close to open, that's the new reality. That was even a worse selloff than we saw in '87 in any stock that I recall. Most stocks in '87 dropped anywhere from 20 to 30% at the most. This stock went down what, 70% in a day? From close to open? Either you had the right position coming in that morning or you were wiped out. To not think that that wasn't the precursor to what can happen in something that is just blown all out of proportion on the bullish side is really fooling yourself. And yet I see institution after institution not hedging, putting other people's money to work – that's another point I wanted to make, too, and I almost forgot – that is probably the reason for the feeling that I have about this being the most dangerous market that I've seen yet. And that is, we have more money today being managed by people whose money it isn't. It's so much easier for them to convince themselves that buying the stock Digital Datawhack trading at fifty times earnings is a safe buy, when its going up, when it goes down the value falls. The point is, emotionally there are no floors or ceilings in euphoria or freefall. If you asked the money manager, "OK, now, would you, yourself, put twenty-five thousand of your own money in that stock right now?" I would say that the majority of them wouldn't even touch it. Why? Well, the answer would be that it's kind of risky. But, take them away from their own money and their own situation and put them in an office in front of a few "machines" and some analysis report on this or that, and they're in there buying that stock with other people's money in size. It's incredible. The whole picture, to me, is just crazy. Once again, it goes back to my trading days when I traded my own money. If I won or lost it, I lost it because it was my own money. The point is, I wasn't trading other people's money, I was trading mine. And there is a big difference between trading your own and trading somebody else's. There's a huge difference. There's a huge emotional difference, and I think there's a definite difference when it comes to using the faculties you develop, faculties that you should be putting to use when it comes to understanding the markets, and I think that that's the lesson that's going to really be learned after all, if I'm right on what the bear market is going to bring about, it is that there's going to have to be some changes. What they're going to be I don't know, but we're going to just have to wait and see just how ugly it gets when the next bear hits.

LE: It'll be fun to look back in a year and a half. Thank you for sharing this with me.

SR: You're welcome.

Chapter 22

Fred Wynia

Fred, where did you get started and did you have any educational background that led you to the market?

Not really, more practical experience than anything else. I started in high school, when the Russians put up the first Sputnik. I had a few dollars saved and my dad introduced me the stock market back in the late 50's. It was pretty easy to make money. You just invested in anything with electronics and it went up. Didn't last too long, but it was a good experience.

You got a gift by following a tip.

Yes, that worked for a while, but they do end eventually and it's not quite as easy as it seems at times. That's how I got started.

How long did you hold whatever you bought? Were you a trader on the first trade you ever did, or were you an investor?

I was always more of an investor, and I can't even remember what rules I had, I didn't really have any, just kept anything that looked interesting. And then I looked at a records report. When you're 16 years old, you don't know much, at least I didn't. I never thought I did. I doubt that it was much more than a brokers report and maybe a word of mouth or a rumor, the kind of stuff the average investor gets involved in. Eventually that kind of logic will not work, except for a short period of time.

I remember my first investment was in American Photocopies because Xerox was going crazy and it was in the same field. I bought it at $15 and a year later sold it at $8.

Well, that was a good experience.

It was a good experience.

You learn some stuff like that. I had just the opposite experience, I had a few hundred dollars in several files and I don't think that is a good experience as a teenager, you just don't learn it, it looks too easy. You're not prepared for the downturns that will come. I had a good time and when I got through college I just had a general business background, and in college I decided I wanted to go into the brokerage business and that's when I got serious about studying the market back in 65-66.

Who were you working with back then?

A firm that is not longer in existence, a firm called Dexy Tober, They were a big N.Y. Stock Exchange. I remember at the time, I started in retail, and gone into a training program and got into trading and got hooked on over the counter market making, which I did eventually do for over 25 years.

Good.

And I got interested in technical analysis after the stock market decline in 1973 & 1974 and wanted to know why markets went bad. I studied seriously and have been using it ever since.

How long have you been with Sherwood securities?

Pretty close to three years. I'm a technical analyst for Sherwood. I give commentaries each morning in a technical meeting to the firm of the various offices to our sales force in NY and the traders coordinated with our research department, the times that we do things together. And I do advise outside clients, people who do business with the firm. Consult to people, but mainly I am focused on doing things for our in house traders and salespeople.

Key things together with the traders, take positions with them, and share information, try to put ideas together, and make money.

What is the source of capital that you trade?

I use firm capital.
So you trade some of their funds, and how do you trade that?

Well, I just have an inventory, like any other trader does, buy and sell things. There is no restrictions on that.

You don't make markets in what you trade?

No.

I see.

Not anymore.

I just invest firm capital, and get paid a percentage of the profits that I make on them. I don't manage money per se, I just invest the firms capital, or a percentage of it.

Do you trade anything other than stocks?

Yes, I can do anything, if I want to. I do play with options. Either with stocks or indices, I could do bonds, but I don't usually. I stick with common stocks and options. I can do it on any exchange, but mostly on OTC. Probably 70% is OTC stocks, and that's the orientation of Sherwood. That's probably the reason.

How many stocks do you think Sherwood markets in?

A couple thousand or more.

What percentage invested are you generally and how many days or weeks are you invested?

That's a hard question. Generally I don't carry very big positions, I do more either day trading or 2,3,4 day type trading because the type of thing I get involved in is volume motivated. So there is usually something going on when I get into it. That starts it, and if it doesn't' take hold right away, I usually flatten it out. Because I made an incorrect decision. It should take place right away.

How many positions do you normally have?

If things were real active, maybe 8 would be the top. Generally, I will have 4 or 5.

So If you had 8 positions you'd be fully invested?

Probably.

Not on margin, but fully invested?

Yes, at least all I want.

How would you describe your style? How do you trade, and how willing are you to make a decision to take the position off or take all of them off depending on the market or whatever?

I am a very quick trader probably because of my background as a market maker. You have to be, you can't be dogmatic about positions that start to go against you. You have to cut losses immediately. There's no reason for me not to do that. No one is looking at me and saying there's too much activity in your account. That's the furthest thing from anyone's mind. The number one motive and reason for watching things closely is to keep the losses small. If something starts to go against me, I'll have some criteria that it has to tick down below a support level or break some kind of resistance level. I give myself some room but generally when I get into something it should move then or I have made a bad decision. If it starts to go the other way, I'll cut losses immediately, that's crucial.

I talked to you when you may have been in your 8 position situation, and the market went south and you went fully to cash. It amazed me that you could be so fluid, but I guess that is part of your background and it allows you to cut the risk.

Yes, if I find it starting to go against me, I will flatten it out quickly. I have some technical guiding forces and tools that I have worked on for years. that will happen quite frequently when I am near my extreme of my indicator, near of overbought so I decide that the string is getting stretched out, or if I sense a flattening out of momentum of the things that I am involved in, I'll get out. I have a hair trigger then because I know that the Market risk is much greater at that time. That's usually what happens when I flatten out everything, I still try to trade stocks on a stock by stock basis, unless there is a market call that is, in my opinion, imminent.

Where does your information come from. How do you decide to trade long or short, on Microsoft for example?

I have a program that I run every night that filters out things I think are set up to buy or sell. For example on the buy side, I'm looking for high relative strength stocks that have pulled back or in the last few days are starting to get over sold. Momentum is starting to come out of the downside pullback and I am looking for a little bit of strength after pullback. My filtering program throws out a list of things like that. On the short side I am looking for things like the weak relative strength side that have rallied up to resistance and have started to flatten out or is starting to roll over. If momentum type things are in play, I have another filter program that will throw out a list of things that are breaking out of trading ranges, on volume or breaking down on volume out of trading ranges. It depends on what I think is going to be most responsive in time and I'll pay more attention to one program or the other.

Information off your computer is where you get your information other than your quote forms?

A lot of times you can get a lot of information out of Investors Daily, if you didn't have anything other than the most advanced volume list you could pick up some ideas out of there. I do that all the time, where something has shown increased strength or volume it happens to be breaking out of a trading range, I might not even have a data base. I have gotten many ideas. You could look at the high list in ID and pick things going into high ground that have got a pretty high share rating. Even if they're not ready to be bought that day, maybe they've gone too far, but you can set up to buy them on some kind of a pullback.

Sounds like you like to buy strong stocks on full rack and sell weak stock on rally?

That's what I do.

What type of info do you get extraneous to Sherwood or your personal computer research or reading? Do you trade ideas with money managers or investors?

I do have a network of people I share ideas with, who provide different types of information than I have. I do that throughout the day. People will call me and I will call people and receive ideas that way. Yes, I do a lot of that.

How do you perform since you've been there, say over the last three years, do you have a monthly goal you try to hit, or an annual goal?

Yes, I do have objectives, sometimes they're more realistic than others, right now the momentum type stocks haven't been a very fruitful type venture, I do a lot in that area, and I have had to cut back my objectives fairly substantially, just to control losses and not let things get out of hand, because you don't get the solitude, at least I find...

So you'd say money made in 1991, 1992, and 1993 was harder?

Yes much more so, for me anyway.

Why do you think that the markets have changed since the last quarter of 1993?

The momentum stocks that were so popular are just not getting the follow through they were. When things would break out you'd get very substantial runs and that is just not the case now. Not that there aren't things that are working, but the number of failures, the things that start to break out and they look OK. It takes more than just momentum players to move stocks. You've got to have real buyers out there, not just people who are going to buy things for a breakout to trade them. There has got to be some legitimate support there. I think you've had a lot of that support going back a year or two, and not nearly so much now. You have to shift as always from sector to sector, depending on what's popular. I think when the techs get out of favor, which they had here up to a month or so ago, you don't get the volatility in basic industry type stock across the board. They will move but you don't get the kind of volatility like you do get in technology or medical or biotech's. Instead of trying to make multi-points, you go for halves or maybe a point. Much smaller trades.

So you're taking smaller positions?

Probably not, probably bigger positions going for less money.

I see. Are you concentrating less on stocks and more on market and options?

I am concentrating more on stocks. I will do the options on the OEX or the midcaps when my technical stuff sets up. That's periodically when I get to extremes on that. I am focused on stocks every day . Long or short, I don't really care, there is stuff to do everyday.

What would you say helped you, (kind of winding this thing up because what we are doing is also going through the test you took for us,) What would you say helped you, I know you don't know any wealthy barbers who get great tips, so what do you think has really helped you the most, and what has hurt you the most?

In terms of tools?

Yes.

I suppose keeping a general market perspective on what I think the market is doing, helps, because I do tend to trade with a bias a little more long or a little more short depending on mode I think were in. Relating bond market movements, I think that's extremely important. I do a lot of work with the bond market even though I may not buy or sell bonds or interest sensitive things specifically, I think that there is so much correlation with equity markets and bond prices that you have to focus on that. I think following that has helped a lot. As far as what hinders me, I am not sure. Maybe at times...

I have never seen you take any real big hits, it seems like the hits you take, you take in stride, is that different from how you've traded over the last few years?

No.

Is it a constant in your line of trading?

I just don't let the losses get out of control. You just address it immediately.

What's out of control? How much of a loss would you take?

Maybe if a $10 stock dropped a point and a half.

You usually don't go 15% do you?

no.

I think you told me more like 4-5%.

Yes, that would be more normal, but if I decided for some reason I wanted to get stubborn and old that that would be out of control; a point and a half.

Would that be allowing the fundamentals to play into your holding of it?

Possibly, but I try not to do that. You just cannot make day to day decisions with fundamentals, it just doesn't work. You make investment decisions and things can be triggered by a fundamental announcement that is a news motivated type thing, trying to make day to day decisions based on something that is in the market already, just doesn't work for trading in my opinion.

You have any particular bias this year, long or short, or are you just going to play what you see without having any opinion?

I think it's always good to have an opinion, but just not to get stubborn and trade day-to-day on those opinions if they're inconsistent with what's happening in the marketplace. I have always got opinions because I've got to advise people who have the long perspective, who are long term investors, but I don't trade with that viewpoint, I'm more interested in the day-to-day. I'll have a point of view that I think the market, like this year I'll be surprised if it is up, I think we are getting stretched out, I think you're seeing lots of excesses in the market, and whether it's going to top out this month or 3 or 4 or 6 months from now I don't really know, but the country funds have made a pretty substantial corrections recently. I think you conceivably had parabolic blowoffs in some of those, and it's not inconceivable to me that the psychology of that is eventually going to affect our market. It hasn't yet, but it certainly could.

So you're saying you don't want too get to heavy on the long side because you fear we might have topped out and if so you don't want to be hit when they pull the plug one day?

Right, I think that's a fair assessment.

On the other hand, you don't just put on shorts because you think that today is the day they're going to fall out of bed, unless they start to fall?

Right. You just trade both sides of the market. Trade stocks and keep things fairly balanced and keep stops tight and under control and you'll make a living. It's just more difficult and not as rewarding as it was a couple of years ago.

It seems like that is certainly the case for me, I am finding that you don't make nearly what we were used to making in January 1992, even.

No.

Well, this is about our normal conversation, it sounds like, we used to talk a lot more, it's gotten harder to make money, so we don't talk as often, I don't have as many ideas to trade, and you don't either.

No, I don't either.

Well, I think we did a good job, so let's conclude it. I'll end up having you sign a release after you've read it, so you're comfortable with what I wrote. Also, John Furey will get your results back to you, and he will do a written profile in three dimensions: what you're dominate in, what you're recessive in, and weaknesses. I think you'll find it fun and interesting. It's pretty informative.

Good.

You may like it enough to have your family do it. I did and it helped me understand why they do things I don't understand. It gives you basic insight into their basic volition and what their choices are. My daughter is very analytical and sometimes I don't understand where she is coming from until I recognize that it is her natural volition to analyze things more than I do. I appreciate the interview and I will get this written up and we will move from there.

Chapter 23

Linda Raschke

Linda Bradford Raschke started trading stocks and options on the Pacific Coast Stock Exchange and later on the Philadelphia Exchange. When I first met Linda ,I was struck by her reflective personality. She is bright and extraordinarily intuitive. I chuckled to myself numerous times since I told her she seemed very intuitive and she whisked my comment aside and said her results were due to following her methodology. I thought, I can hardly wait to see the results of her test profile——I knew she would be off the chart in measurement of intuition (She Was).

Linda, in the manner of a discerning trader, focuses on a few commodities. Based on past observations and experiences she studies what patterns re setting up. When Linda sees a pattern [buy or sell] her sense is not based on penetrating vision but rather her expertise sees a rapid conclusion xyz is [buy or sell]. Linda does not trudge to a conclusion step by step. The apparent inexplicability in her discretionary entry/exit is that it involves a substantial change in understanding that occurs in a brief interval of time and without detectable explicit reasoning.

LE: How did golf evolve? what is it and what rules did you look for in that golf system?

LR: Well, I just observed certain tendencies in the market. Now, maybe this will be more along those lines of intuition you talked about, Lin, OK? But, through your observations, you note that there are certain behavior characteristics of the market, and what you're trying to do is find a way to take advantage of a repetitive pattern that sets up.

So, with something like the Golf system, I say "Here's a pattern. How can I take advantage of it?" For example, let's say the market in the afternoon, if there's strong direction in the afternoon, at some point it has a tendency to have some type of follow-through the next day. That would be a very simple thing, and what you have to do is find a robust, non-optimized type of way with very simple rules and parameters to take advantage of that. And the idea is that you only want to get a little piece, but a very high percentage of the time. So, I'm very much into the hitting singles kind of game. Knock it out, knock it out. blind it out, blind it out, and I'm one of those people who have to have high percentage ratio, because I like that constant reinforcement of succeeding. If I feel like I'm going to fail in a game, I more or less refuse to play. That's why I don't like going to the casinos or playing games of chance or something like that. If I don't know that I can win, I don't want to play.

Golf system says if its going my way, buy based on today's apparent closing trend with a strong likelihood of a strong opening tomorrow and sell that strength. Then you go out and play "GOLF".

LE: You also mentioned in your record, something in the last three years, you only had a two percent draw down or something like that.

LR: That's from the beginning of this year.

LE: Oh, this year, Ok.

LR: On a daily basis, but, part of that is just because I've been trading much more conservatively this year in terms of, my whole goal in trading this year has been to eliminate stress from our life, and now my object has been, what is the least stressful way to trade? What is the way that I can trade day after day and never experience an adrenaline rush? Whereas, a lot of my trading in the eighties, I would say I was very aggressive and I was very profitable. But, it also came at a price. I would have much more volatility and much more stress and that may have been one of the reasons why I just finally hit the wall, because I'd drive myself a hundred and ten percent of the time...

LE: And, finally, your body said, "That's enough. Stop it.."

LR: My body said, "I can't take this anymore."

That's like when I had Erika and we were redoing this house and here I am with a newborn child and I'm still in there trading a hundred and ten percent every day, and I just never took time off.

I had to learn to set limits in my own lifestyle, and that was something I had never ever done. Growing up, my Mom, and the way my parents raised me, it's always like mind over matter. You can do anything you want to. One of these very encouraging, supportive...

LE: Type A personality..

LR: Right, so I just assumed that you should be able to do a million things at once. And my Mom is very much that way. She's got four kids, works full time, does this, does that, does typing, backpacking, very active type of lady...

LE: Sky's the limit...

LR: Yeah, exactly. So, I had to make some changes.

LE: So, to sum up what you said, would you say that you have changed your style into a lower risk, higher probability, selective mode and, because of that, you're now trading with less stress?

LR: Much less stress, but I would say that I tend to just take the trades that play it safe, whereas, before, I would take a lot of trades with which coordinates would show promise. In other words, by being aggressive on the entry, it would have a very high payoff. But, there might be a lower probability of it working out in an hour, day, or week. And, now, I tend to only take the high probability trades. But, they always have a much lower risk reward ratio. The payoff is only two to one as opposed to ten to one.

LE: You're not trying to do the home run. You're doing singles and consistency.

LR: Right, very much so, and it's less profitable for me because I had a very good return on those home runs. Or, look at it this way. I'd be playing in a very volatile market. Now, if there's too much volatility, I kind of tend to just back off. Small positions, less intense involvement.

LE: What market, to you, have you found to be the most profitable? We talked about...

LR: For me, it's always S & P and then the currencies and then the bonds. Pretty much the financial futures, for me. But, anything related to the index futures or markets, because that's my background. I had all those years of trading stocks and options and that's really my forte. I'm very good at reading the market in the tape.

LE: You're in the process now of putting together a partnership, or raising money?

LR: Um, in a...

LE: You don't have to say anything about any of this...

LR: No, that's Ok.

I'm trying to keep it small and exclusive. I don't want to get so big that I lose my flexibility. You see? There is that option, right? I know that once you try managing a hundred million dollars or two hundred million dollars, all of a sudden there are certain markets you can't trade. You can't do market orders in certain markets. You get a lot more restrictions just because of your size, and, if you notice, almost every CTA that had hundred percent returns on ten million dollars, when they start trading a hundred million dollars, all of a sudden, they're only making twenty-five percent returns.

So, I have this philosophy that there's a niche in the marketplace for every type of player and I would like to deal more with high returns, higher incentive fees, exclusive business, and try to optimize my returns with a lesser amount of money. In other words, there is a curve, and I want to find the most efficient spot on the curve for me to maximize my returns, which I believe, for me, is staying at the low end of the curve, in terms of the dollar amount that I manage.

Because I can have higher returns for the client.

There's a certain point where you start managing a hundred million dollars, and, all of a sudden, you're hiring more employees, you're hiring accountants, you're hiring attorneys, and it's a lifestyle. You're that much more involved in non-trading tasks, also, which I don't want to be. I want to be involved, only, one hundred percent in trading tasks, not too much the overall management parts of the business.

So, I feel like I've given a lot of thought as to exactly how I want to run my business.

LE: And, you now have someone who is assisting you, I understand.

LR: Right.

LE: How does that help?

LR: A couple of ways. It's just nice to have another compatible person in the room, number one. I think it keeps it just a little more focused, because I guess I would have been concentrating a little bit less from the burnout factor, and it takes some of the load off your shoulders. Somebody else can watch for slip-ups or monitor trades, these type of activities. In trading there's absolutely no room for sloppiness.

One mistake, or one oversight, you forget one thing, it can cost you dearly.

If you don't put a trade down, you find the next day that you were long or short and the market's going to get you.

If an error slips into your account that you don't notice, and you don't resolve it right away, it becomes a bigger problem later on, or you forget that you had a resting stop out in one market that accidentally gets filled. These silly little things that can happen, there's really no room for that in running your business.

LE: What would you say is your instinctive make-up in terms of how you operate? Do you analyze fundamentals? Do you read a lot of research?

LR: I don't analyze fundamentals. I guess I try and instinctively try and find something that 's out of line in my little universe. For example, if I have a model of behavior in my head, and price overshoots too far, or retraces too far, something like that, I guess, technically, you would say that it's more regression analysis back to the mean, buying what I feel is fair value, and then selling it out when somebody wants to pay too much for it.

LE: How does your instinctive make-up enter into that skill?

LR: I think, from being on the trading floor, you get a very good sense of when the markets became very irrational, and people would become misguided in how they were pricing things. Or, would start acting irrationally, either out of panic or fear or way over paying for something. I guess what I like to see is more when markets have gotten a little too speculative. You have to be careful in playing a contrary game, because you never want to be fading the smart money of the big boys and the large institutional stuff. But, when you see the public involved in a high degree, that's where you kind of smell the blood.

LE: You mentioned in previous interviews that have been published that you do your homework at night off of a trade sheet and you follow yesterday's price activities, or, as the case might be, tonight's price activities looking for tomorrow's move, whether it's a breakout of yesterday's price area, or whether you're going to take a counter trend move. How do you know tonight how you're going to trade tomorrow?

LR: I never know for sure. I mean, you can just set up this is the way I should be trading, but then you always have to let the markets tell you or dictate what they're truly going to do. So, you still have to leave yourself that flexibility to change your game plan mid-stream. But, I find that if you, at least, approach the market with the game plan, that is better than nothing at all. So, when I'm looking to be in a slim trading mode or a breakout mode, a lot of it's going to have to do with the degree of contraction in a market. I have quantified parameters or objectives, parameters to establish the guidelines by. When the range is contracting a certain amount, or another thing that I look is when a lot of my momentum oscillators have stopped oscillating, it would be very analogous to seeing a chart, a triangle formation on a chart.

You don't want to be playing as those triangles approach the point of the triangle, because the prediction for the breakout becomes fifty-fifty. You can't predict direction. All you know is that you can predict that there's going to be a volatility expansion.

LE: Are you talking about price on the chart, or the oscillator?

LR: Well, both...price and the oscillators will tend to form triangles or contractions or rising wedges or whatever the case may be.

So that signals to you that there's possibly a change in trend occurring because the volatility has gone out on the downside or the upside and there's support or resistance.

You don't know if it's going to be a change of trend or a continuation. That's my whole point. You can't predict the direction. There are certain formations of patterns that, statistically, you cannot predict the directional outcome with any edge. So, if I can't back test it and come out and predict the direction with a greater than a sixty or sixty-five percent confidence, more or less, then that's when I would go into a breakout mode. I can't predict the direction, therefore, I'm not going to play unless the market pulls me in with some sort of momentum.

LE: So, if you're looking at price and you can observe a triangle or a wedge building there, and you're looking at an oscillator, what do you see next?

LR: That's when you have to stop looking at the oscillators, you see...

You cannot look at oscillators in these types of contractions, or triangles are totally irrelevant, because they'll pull back down to the half way mark, and they can go either way. They'll just start oscillating around the central value, and like the amplitude will flatten out. There's nothing there to read. There are only two main times you can't look at oscillators. You can't look at oscillators in a strongly trending market, and you can't look at oscillators in a market that's not oscillating. Right? There's nothing to measure. So, that's where you have to go into a mode, where if the market's going to do something, it'll usually break out with some type of expansion in range or momentum or some other indicator like that. And that's when you say, Ok, well, if the market's going to move, it's got to move strong enough that it's going to come up and get me. You have to look at today's closing data and plan for tomorrow. I write it down on a trade diary.

LE: Then you'll buy the strength..

LR: Exactly..

or sell the weakness.

LE: Ok, what have been your observations about divergences .

LR: Well, divergent tools, I would say that, intuitively, can stop a loss of momentum and a loss of acceleration in the market and a divergence is just simply measuring that objectively with an oscillator, Ok? But, intuitively, as a trader, even if you weren't looking at oscillators, you can sense that second leg up on lesser open interest and lesser volume or lesser momentum readings. That is definitely something that you can feel as a trader, and the oscillators will just measure it objectively and usually the most I will look for out of a divergence is just a simple correction. It doesn't necessarily imply that there's a trend change. It just implies a simple correction. So, it's a trade. There's a divergence and you feel it. You confirm it with a technical indicator just to make a trade.

LE: Ok, so you make the trade, say you do it late in the day...

LR: Ok...

Say you saw a divergence, you saw, possibly, price goes to a new high and, or you saw, maybe, the oscillator diverging from price.

LE: And you decide, Ok, the price is going up, you want to take the trade, what do you use the next day to get you out if it goes in your direction that day and do you go home with a profit on the trade? What are you going to use to take you out tomorrow morning, since you went in on a diversion?

LR: Well, let's assume that you're just trading off of a daily bar chart and you have a divergence set up, your holding period depends on the term the oscillator is, the longer term you can hold the trade. In other words, if I'm taking a divergence off of an intermediate term oscillator, I know that I can expect to hold that trade for four to six days. If I'm taking a divergence off of a very short term time frame, a two day rate of change or something, although I can only expect to hold that trade a day or two. If I'm taking a divergence that's been building up in the market for awhile, I mean, I know that maybe I can hold that trade for months. You kind of let the market tell you as you go along. In other words, a divergence has an expected behavioral response and that is that if your divergence is a good trade the market should crack very quickly. Ok? In other words, you don't have a situation where you put on a trade because there's a divergence and have the market go sideways for four days. That's a big red warning bell to close out that trade, because the market didn't crack and it should. So, you have to say, when the market does sell off, let's say I sold on this divergence, how strong is the selloff? In other words, you're always letting the market tell you whether you should be closing out the trade or holding it for continuation and it's strictly a factor of how long is the move, how strong is the move, how severe is the move and, generally, the more severe the move, the longer you can hold the trade.

LE: So, when you say you're allowing your intuition to override the divergence, if the divergence goes sideways, you went into it for a fall and it didn't occur, the market's now going sideways. And, if the divergence is still in place...

LR: It's now, you keep on saying, intuition, I guess, from repeated observations and statistical testing, that there should be an expected response to confirm the trade, Ok?

You put on a divergence and when they start selling off and making new two-day lows, that's your confirmation that the trade is good.

LE: Alright!

LR: If you feel every trade has 1) a setup condition and 2) a confirmation and 3) an outcome. Then by just seeing a divergence, all you're seeing is the setup, so you put the position on in anticipation that you will get confirmation that it's a good trade. If you don't get that confirmation within an expected time window, you have no confirmation that it's a good trade, and you'd better get out. You have to think of it in terms of steps. On anticipating this condition, here's the setup for it now, here's the trigger for my entry, here's the confirmation that it's a good trade, and here's where I'm out type of thing.

If that sequence gets interrupted along the way, you'd better get out of the trade.

LE: Do you override some of the oscillators based on your historical experiences?

LR: It's not that you're overriding the oscillators. There are just certain times where they're not an appropriate tool in the market place. No tool is appropriate a hundred percent of the time because you can't have one tool that measures market conditions exactly all the time. One tool may be appropriate in a sideways market. Another tool may be appropriate in a trending market. So, that may be where the judgment factor comes in. What type of market conditions are we in, therefore, what tools should I be using? You can quantify that and you can look at it subjectively.

I have found that for myself, even though I may have an intuition, I can't trade in the market off the seat of my pants or just off intuition, because I'll start to get into trouble that way because then you have to recognize, well, when is your intuition good and when is your intuition bad. You can't put that kind of mental pressure on yourself. So, I say to myself, I guess the times I allow my pure intuitions to come into play is when not to take a signal off my system.

I have a feeling that this signal is not going to be a good one. I'm not going to take it. That's where I use my intuition. But, I really try not to let pure intuition get me into a trade. I might have an intuition or a feeling about something, but I will always go to a technical model or look for some type of confirmation that's an objective pattern.

LE: You said system a minute ago, and I'm wondering, how would you describe what you call your system as opposed to... It seems like you do a lot of observing, and the night before you decide, well, looks like this might be a swing trade or a trend trade, or could be a breakout trade tomorrow?

LR: I'm looking for the setups within my actual triggers and entries and rules in my system that are all defined by certain momentum conditions.

LE: So, your system is not like a black box where you buy above the opening or sell below the opening at a specified...

LR: No, not at all, because it does have very specific rules and guidelines. In other words, let's just say that you always wanted to be on the right side of the pivot point or something like that. It's not going to tell you when to get out or when to get in, but you want to stay on the right side of this trend or this line, or this...

LE: A pivot point would be an area where there is less resistance in one direction than another because of the setup that's worked through support or resistance through a point where...

LR: I mean, the pivot point that I use is the strict mathematical calculation. It's just a guideline. I mean, a pivot point could be anything you want. It's just like, for example, let's say your pivot point is the previous day's low, and you always want to be trading higher than that previous day's low. You see, there's no magic in that particular number. It's just saying that you don't want to be trading in a market that's making lower lows than it made yesterday from the long side, even though it might be a great trade to buy it lower, I'd rather and only trade when it's trading higher than the previous day's low. That would be a very simple rule that may not be the optimal rule out there. But, for me, it's easy to understand, it's easy to work with. It has to be very simple for me to deal with it. I do not believe in all of these space networks and stuff, my trading has to be conceptually pure and simple and logical.

Yes, and that would be a very logical rule. Only trade higher than the previous day's high on the long side. If I'm going to be trading the short side, I'm only going to be trading it when the price action is lower than the previous day's high. That's a very safe way to limit your losses and keep you out of trouble, and keep you from picking tops and those types of things.

So, in other words, a market might sell off some and I'll look to sell the first rally, as long as it doesn't exceed the previous swing high. That would be a very simple rule. That's pretty much the essence of my trading. I like to be selling low or highs and buying high or lows, and whichever swing is the longest in length is the direction that I like to play.

In other words, if the market pulls back five points, but rallies ten points, I want to be able to play the long side...

As a constant trend buyer and

As backing into the trend. Looking for the pull backs in the direction of the trend.

Back to what I was saying is that there are certain times when you can use oscillators and certain times, right here you can see that we've gone through a big, long contraction through a sideways movement. This is what I was talking about with the points of triangles and they've just broken out, and you can see the oscillators are of no use whatsoever. They just hover around...

Zippo...

You might just as well throw them out the window and go into what I was calling a breakout mode, which is actually what we did on Friday. We actually did buy sugar as it was breaking out.

LE: Where, to you, is the pivot point on that? Right where your arrow is, is where I see it. Right where it was. It's the blue line, just about.

LR: Well, on this actual one, it was based on taking the previous day's range and adding it. It had to expand a certain amount beyond that previous day's range.

LE: You see it differently than I do, then. My background in stocks would say the pivot point is essentially...

LR: You're drawing a trend line...

LE: Yes, it's basically drawing a trend line. Someplace where that blue arrow is. It is a spot where it has met resistance and now has broken trend resistance.

LR: There is no right or wrong pivot point. The point is that when you're in the breakout mode, you're going with the mood. You could have a simple rule such as buying new highs made after the first hour, or buying afternoon strength, or it can be a certain price function. It doesn't matter what it is. The point is, you're going with the strength and not against it. Any breakout method will get you in on a move like that.

It doesn't matter what method you use. If it's a legitimate breakout, it's going to get you in.

So, in this type of top flat, totally sideways market, where these oscillators lose their oscillations, they're obviously of no value.

It's a beautiful triangle mode. I did add to it and I added to it at higher prices.

It held, and because it hadn't met my rules for exiting, I'm not having to make judgments, do I get in or get out, it's following a system type of thing.

That's the forty-bar simple period moving average, right. I use that and I use a twenty period exponential, and for here it broke out again, and what we'll do is we'll probably exit half the position on Monday morning. But, usually, after you get...

LE: Is that your three day rule?

LR: Well, for this particular trade, you used up a lot of bullets on Friday and what'll happen, is if it gaps open, or it does morning strength, it'll have to pull back, and we can re-buy it back. But, you're only going to get so much at once type of thing.

Sugar has it's pretty big tendency of using up all its bullets in one day, you see...

Now, this day, this wasn't very big. It definitely can have more upside, especially since you just had such a really nice long basing period.

As a general rule of thumb, the longer the consolidation, the better the move you'll get out of that.

But, you don't particularly measure that to look for an objective...

I don't like looking for numerical objective points because I find that they never test out with any statistical accuracy. You can get a rough idea, but way too often it doesn't meet those objectives, or it far exceeds them.

And, so, what I will get is, let me put up another indicator here which is...

This is like a short term two day rate of change. And, if I'm... let's put the S&P because it's a little more dramatic... I always go, it's just a mechanical way or mathematical way or representing the length of the swing. So, in this case, the length of the swing was down, you made new momentum lows here, right? And it would be my first instinct at this point to be selling the first rally, to look for some time of retracement, or double bottom, you see, in the oscillator. I look for double bottoms in this just like would in the charts, so, as it turns out, you made new momentum highs which re-indicated that the trend was up.

This is probably about a ten percent occurrence that you get new lows followed by new highs.

LE: You mean in the indicator, but not in the index.

LR: Right. But, still, it said that this was a strong enough move to negate the beginning of any down trend, ok? Now, here you see a momentum breakout, if you don't look at the actual charts. See, I don't like looking at the charts because I can't read anything.

We had a new momentum breakout to the upside, so you buy the first pullback. At this point you can see the divergence. It's set up on this little short term rate of change and that's why we did take a short...

We got short on this day here at 462. We sold it on that day at 462 and we just ended up covering it the next day at 458. So, we got just four points in our pocket. And those are the types of trades that I like to look for, whereas I can go in real quick and grab a piece and not mess with the choppy junk.

LE: Good trade...

LR: I think that during this whole period, there was just one S&P trade. It was just too flat.

During the whole month, or whatever that is, only two and one-half weeks.

I didn't make any trade at all because there wasn't anything to trade. So, I'll try and stay out of markets like that.

And I have rules, like here's a good rule pattern. This is how I use oscillators. This red line is your middle line. In fact, I can even show it better...

It's just a zero line. You can call it the mean in this particular case. Remember how I was showing you on that sugar part how I was using the oscillator rallies to sell retracements. If I just take this line and this is a sixteen period moving average of this oscillator, no big deal, and this will work on any oscillator. You can take a longer moving average of it. You can make simple little rules.

I've made a simple little rule like when this dotted line, when the moving average is below the zero line, all I'm going to be doing is selling rally. And, when this dotted line is above the zero line, all I'm going to be doing is buying dips.

LE: Because your trend is above the average...

LR: Simple. See?

Trade in the right direction...

So, here it's negative, you're selling the rally, and here you could say you're buying the dips, and to me it's just so much easier to do it off of this where you've got really set rules as opposed to trying to interpret the charts. Well, is this a breakdown below the moving average or not, or, that type of thing.

Now, here would be a case, let's say I sold this piece here because the dotted line is lower, right? So, let's say I sold this and I would have set rules for this. Ok, here's the price you can see that after five days I didn't get anything, so I'd get out of the trade. And, usually, when you trade this way, you find that you can use pretty tight stops using the last swing high or swing low. I mean, that's what I really like to use, the last swing high or last swing low. I mean, it makes trading ever so simple, you're buying the pullbacks to line, right?

Even here, you can still buy the pullback or get a good trade out of that, buying the dips each time and so you have like a very simple system, to me that's a system, ok...

    LE: So you're playing on the long side up here and on the short side..

    LR: Down here, uh huh, and there's one other rule that I use, and that's going into a slump. If this is a downward slope, I'd sell rally, and if it's a rising slope, you buy dips. So, here, in this case, I could sell that piece because this is a strong downward slope.

    LE: That's great...

    LR: Same configuration, same rule...it works on a five minute time frame. In fact obviously, you're in an up trend the whole time here. Without even looking at the chart, you can see you're always above the level... As long as this purple line is above the red line, I'm going to be looking to buy dips. Here's the first time that I can sell. I can sell here because I've got a downward slope.

    LE: What is that, a five minute chart?

    LR: It's five minutes.

I could sell here because I've got a downward slope. I could sell here, because I've got a downward slope. But, it's a marginal, it's not a great sale. You'd get...

This was a good sell point here, because it went from down to even, down a point twenty, and realistically, if you brought half of that, sixty cents, you have a couple of hundred bucks there. I mean, for what, twenty minutes work? So, I mean I will go against the trend, too.

    LE: If you're looking for one trade a day and you see it crossing the red line, near the opening, I guess that is...

Or coming into the opening, isn't it?

    LR: Right.

It never broke down here, it stayed in our range. It looks like here is where you want to take your long and then someplace in here is like where you're talking about selling it.

And that's still in line with your average, which is Okay.

Although, sideways consolidations usually resolve themselves in the directions of the trade, and usually you never even pull back to the moving average. All you do is to get ahead of yourself a little bit and come back to fair value at the time, which is like the moving average.

Uh huh, and that's another one you can add to.

LE: Yeah.

LR: So, here is a chart of the...oh, it's not going to be any good.

I can't find a nice, good, volatile market.

Oh, here it is, sugar.

See what I was saying about how, when you get these breakouts, they tend to occur very quickly? You can't waste the time. You pick up the phone and you get in.

We ended up adding, right here, we got filled at nine seventy-two, seventy-three, seventy-four, seventy-five. We got filled all in this area. That's why, being in a breakout mode means you either have to have your order resting out there, ready to jump on board. You can't hesitate, Right? He, who hesitates is lost and left in the dust.

LE: And that's why you have to do your lists the night before, to tell you to get ready.

LR: Right.

Here would have been a nice little trade.

Just let me put up a, just for fun, put up an hourly chart.

That's a good move for that, isn't it? Three cents?

LE: I like that red line idea. It's like a speed trap.

LR: Same thing here. It's like you probably would have been pretty much buying dips, buying dips and you could use the moving average as confirmation, as long as you're above that, and try to pull back to the moving average, which is pretty steady.

These little things are the night sessions here which is spastic.

LE: They must be hitting stops that somebody, or whatever, there...same market.

LR: Yeah, here's your daily chart. You had a really good buying off of two ninety right there.

Here, you're just starting to come up. It would have been a lot safer to buy right here. See, at this point, this is the way I like to do it. I like to buy a higher low. This is the lowest low here, so in my book you don't have any new confirmed up trends. Even at this point, because you made a new higher high, it doesn't confirm that there's an up trend. You have to have both a higher high and a higher low and then you can see there's an up trend. This could be just like an expanding triangle that can involve itself on the downside again.

If I were trading in this type of area, I would only be looking to hold the trade for two or three days. If I'm long, I don't have any trend, I'm just doing a scalp. That's why you're saying how long you hold the trade really depends on how supportive the overall structure is.

Now, I'll show you my best trade of the last month. This is my best trade of the last month! We bought. We added one unit here and we bought the second unit here on the tenth. You see, this is my favorite pattern. You come down, rally up and pull back and test. You see, you have like a nice double bottom there. That is my all time favorite pattern. The last pattern you can use with this exchange is the divergence, which, in this case...

With your red line...

LE: Yeah...

LR: Keeps you honest, here...

I showed you two cases where you can buy the dips because they are higher lows. Or, you can buy it because it's got a rising moving average, I mean a rising slope, right? and the last case, which I haven't told you about, yet, but I'm going to now, is where you have a divergence that usually happens ten days apart. See, that's my complete rule book, and

I actually charged people twelve hundred dollars to learn that from me at a course in Denver.

So, here you have it, the complete Linda Raschke guide to trading, Okay? (1) A divergence, (2) a slope, (3) positive or negative moving average. That's all you need.

LE: You don't have the slope going for you on that trade, yet.

LR: No, you don't. You'll never have all three. You'll rarely even have two. This is a rare case, right there, where you have slope and positive moving average.

LE: What was your third thing to test?

LR: A divergence.

You've got divergence, you've got the moving average, and what else?

You've got the slope and whether it's positive or negative. All that's written down for you.

LE: I've got it written right here in this tape!

LR: Whether the moving averages are above or below the zero line, whether it's sloping up or down or whether it's divergence, that's all you need to know. So, we did, right here. We bought at nine fifty-five. We established our position, but I knew it was going to come out here very strong, so we held it all the way up and we exited in our position at eleven sixty on Thursday. That has got to be my best trade.

LE: It looks like a twenty percent move, and what kind of return on the...

LR: Well, one contract, if you go from nine fifty to ten fifty is a thousand dollars. That was two thousand dollars and margin I know was under two thousand dollars. It was greater than a hundred percent return on margin.

LE: A hundred percent in a month?

LR: Yeah!

Not bad for a week.

LE: take it!

LR: And see how you you're making your second top up here and you have like a possible divergence, I mean it was just a good time to exit. It was a great time to get out. Also, here's another long term trade I did.

Coffee. It's like triangles are starting to form here and I got long coffee in this area. I started holding it, and I did hold it here through the market sloppiness. I knew I was putting it on as a long term trade... Here's the weeklies, the weeklies have, at this point, a higher low right here, and that was like the first higher or low you had had on a weekly chart in ages, okay, for a continuation. Forget that this was like a contract rollover type of thing. But, it was like the first time in the weeklies that it was a nice powerful pattern. Don't worry, I'll show you my buy sheets.

So, I did buy there. I was holding my breath here that it wouldn't make a new low and I stayed long all the way up to here. I got stopped out right here. We started making the first low. We got stopped out here. And we bought on this day here.

LE: Why did you re-buy it?

LR: Because we were still in the up trend. It was still...

LE: You couldn't close the gap.

LR: Right. This purple line... You can see, it was a great buy signal, it was like a great buying opportunity, a perfect pullback from the moving average and a bunch of things, so I rebought there, stayed with it, stayed with it, stayed with it. I ended up getting stopped out on that day at half my position. I got out half of it, but I never bought back the other half. I'm still long half of it. So, that's my flaws, that I've got shaken out a little bit there and now I'm only long half of what I was. That's the only other really long term trade that I have...recently.

LE: You've been in that two weeks, it looks like.

LR: Yeah.

LE: That's been a really good trade.

LR: Here's where I get tripped up. This is why I say don't stay in flat, choppy markets that aren't doing anything, because I can tell you that's what always, always, always costs me.

Let's see, again, points of triangles. You can't predict points of triangles.

I think there's a divergence there, maybe there's not. See how this thing just gets flat and unreadable...

LE: Not a good market to be in.

LR: No, I bought it thinking it was making a triangle here and you were going to come out the upside and I got stopped out.

LE: The slope of your moving average is down, too, from over here.

LR: Right, but see, I was counting that as just having turned up it was going to pull everything up and it was a higher low and all that kind of stuff. You can't do it.

LE: That's a non-trend market.

LR: I was in my breakout mode here and I got a buy stop. I got stopped into the trade here. We didn't get out. We probably should have, and we ended up getting stopped out here.

LE: Still not a bad loss, though.

LR: No, they're little losses, but it's like it's very aggravating. I shouldn't be playing in this market at all. It's a waste of time. See, those tend to be the things, that if I could just keep myself out of these stupid markets...

LE: But, if you went back to your rules, you knew that wasn't where you should be in, just by your own...

LR: We got into corn, we started building a position up in corn, it looked like everything was turning up here, somewhere in here, we bought and we ended up getting out of it all on that date. I reversed and I think we took like a two cent loss, which isn't big, but you know we were in a lull trade. We were in the trade probably for a week and it went nowhere, and then it pulled down, I'm glad I got out when it did break down. I probably should have gone short, but I didn't.

We got in and got out. It doesn't matter. With markets, when there's nothing happening, you can't read them, but sometimes I look at this and, the longer term structural pattern, and I'll say, look, you made this really nice big triangle here and there's an opposite coming, I see one, two corrections, here, and these odds that it can come out the up side after that, so sometimes I'll just wait to see if we can get some continuation going, which you couldn't. So, that's knowing myself, that I'll have a tendency to want to get into these triangles, and I know it's my weakness. I'll get in and something happens and I'll end up taking my two cents loss.

LE: Well, thank you for the Bermuda Triangle.

LR: That is, that is a good, I like that terminology, the Bermuda Triangle.

It's something to steer clear of.

LE: Fun trading with you.

LR: Thanks!At home in Philadelphia with Linda Bradford Raschke October 1993

Linda started trading stocks and options on the "P" Coast Stock Exchange and later the Philadelphia Exchange. When I first met Linda, I was struck by her reflective personality. She seemed bright and extraordinarily intuitive. I chuckled to myself numerous times since I told her she seemed very intuitive and she whisked my comment aside and said her results were the result of sales and following her system path. I thought, I can hardly wait to see the results of her test profile – I knew she would be off the chart in intuition (SHE WAS).

Linda, in the manner of a very discerning trader, focuses on 20 commodities. Based on past observations and experiences she refines what patterns are setting part and programs her computer to advise her when to take the trades.

Chapter 24

Tom O'Malley

LIN: Tom, you and I have worked together for about a year, yes?

TOM: A year plus, I think.

LIN: OK, I've traded with you on the basis of your understanding of your firm's research, and you've acted as a sales trader/analysts.

TOM: Yes, that's fair, definitely a trader.

LIN: What is your educational background that led you to this job?

TOM: I went to a private high school in Greenwich CT, and then I graduated from Boston College with an economics degree. I have always been involved in the stock market since I was 12 or 13. I have always been interested in it, and known stocks in some way or other.

LIN: That's a similarity that you haven't shared with me. I also had that same experience.

TOM: Yes, I have been involved with the market for a long time, and that kept me involved with it through high school and also into college. After graduating from college, I was offered a job at American Express in the Finance Training Program. In hindsight, I should have just gone straight to Wall Street. I worked three summer jobs at Wall Street. I worked at Newberger-Berman, which is a big money management outfit, and I should have just gone there, but American Express had a big name program and a pretty prestigious program so I figured I'd just go there. It was a good experience, as I learned how inefficient a big company could possibly be. I learned a lot of number crunching; I did a lot of bank analyses, which helped in really understanding the analysis of the stocks. From there I went...

LIN: Did you ever trade commodities?

TOM: Through the family, my old man was an oil trader for a long time, still is, and I went from American Express to Louis Dreyfuss Energy, which is a commodity-trading firm. I traded commodities for a few months, but my real love and desire was in the stock market and I kept always focusing on the stock market and not worrying about what oil or silver or whatever was doing. I concentrated more on stocks so I figured I should be in the market. Now today, we trade a little commodities on the side. A group of three guys who do the futures, do a little oil, and do a little of the currencies. It's very small. My focus and concentration, 98% of my day is in the stocks.

LIN: What about options, is that a sore subject?

TOM: Options, it has been lately. They say that 70% of the people don't make money options. I was one of the 70% this month. I consider the options, when I get more capital I will be more intent on selling some calls naked. Currently I play options from the long side. I also write a lot of covered calls on the positions I like. Usually I will buy the common, if I like the stock I will press a bet with the options.

LIN: I seems lately, over the past year, the first part of last year you could make money and you could press the options along with the stock positions and be in momentum. Last year, in October into January of 94, it's been harder to play that game because the movements in the stocks gets abated pretty quickly.

TOM: Yes, I agree, I came quickly out of the shoot last year. Made a lot of money in big hits. I actually made no money October & November and I gave up money, as I owned concentrated positions and they fell off, then they picked up toward the end of the year. This year I came fast out of the shoot, I had some real nice goals, but then you saw with the CA. That really hurt. It was classic, we were on a roll, like the story, the company had disappointed, so it would seem prudent to press the debt, unfortunately the company's reporting, and the way they reported, confused me. I think it will be tough to get the nice hits we got last year.

LIN: The Dow has been an easy place to be and stay, but that doesn't seem the kind of thing that you and I follow.

TOM: No the Dow is...I was just talking with someone else who was yelling at me because we haven't made any cyclical calls, and we have a couple of analysts, Jim Dalhling, who is the traveling and basically covers the transportation areas. He hasn't made a whole lot of calls on the rails and the rails have been a good place to be. Obviously the Autos have been a good place to be. We have that call, but that's kind of an all-call. The Dow hasn't been a place that I have focused. In the market the last few weeks, you had the Dow making new highs, and S&P not doing anything. Today is the first day where you get a broader range of the Dow being up 10 and the S&P being up 2 1/2 almost 3. It's not the stocks you and I have been playing in and I am actually pretty hungry for cyclicals right now. Open to ideas. The technology ploys that we're playing are good last year. It feels like they're running out of steam on some of them, on others which we should be long have been short plays, and they are getting squeezed to death now. The power softs of the world of 30-54. That type of thing.

LIN: What type of accounts do you talk to?

TOM: A broad spectrum. I have my standard trading accounts, like you, probably 5 people like you I call up and they respond right away, assuming the story sounds good. Then I have semi-traders and holds where they hold it either for the event or a little longer term. Earnings, that type of thing. And then they are willing to buy a little more if the earnings keep up. They build a position off of that. The traders are either all fundamental or technical or they combine the two. The middle group-more fundamental and technical, they will buy on the fundamental assuming the chart looks OK but they don't spend a lot of time on the chart. Then I come to very traditional, bigger hedge firms that act more like institutions, where instead of talking to one or two people, like I call you up and you do the trade, they talk with their analysts. The response is not as quick. They come in and buy a big size afterward. I cover a big array of accounts, that's important. You have to be up on the stories. When the stories don's work, for example on the CA trade, the stock got hit, you're willing to stand in there if you understand the fundamentals. I spent time with two one-on-ones with other money management places, went to lunch with CA, I am familiar with the fundamentals and the reason I am is I cover these more institution oriented accounts where they really want to know the down and dirty fundamentals.

LIN: So they can sleep at night if it goes against them, although that doesn't' mean a thing. Whereas, in the past we might have taken less than a 10% loss, now if we understand the story, we are more comfortable hanging in.

TOM: Right. Obviously it is no longer a very short-term thing. The other advantage we had in this situation is that it wasn't hugely expensive.

LIN: It will be interesting to see how your personal profile you filled out conveys your analytical ability and you intuitive side, which is your trading side. To see if you have the balance that you think you have. I will be anxious to see that.

TOM: That will be interesting.

LIN: You don't do much on the short side do you?

TOM: No, I am optimistic about life so I tend to go for the long. I will not do valuation shorts. I'll short something if I've done a lot of work on the story and I'm getting indications from other people that business is slowing down. If something is fundamentally wrong then I will look to sell it short. If I do sell something short I will not withstand as much pain as I will if I'm on something. That I really do just for a trade. I'll cover it, an example is Storage Tech. I was short that. Short around 33 34 1/2, I felt like it was running against me, a lot of people were covering. Although I still feel like it was a fundamental short, that's not where I have made money in the past. I think, in the future it will be where I make a little more money. I have to be honest, I want to get into it slowly.

LIN: How do you use your general market perspective in terms of correlating stocks? Do you spend any time thinking about timing stocks?

TOM: About timing the stocks or timing the market?

LIN: Both.

TOM: I like to time stocks based on trading something, based on an earnings release, or the fundamentals getting better. As far as the market goes, it's tough to say. Over the past 3 years the market could go against you, yet still make money, as long as the fundamentals come through. I remember last week we traded on that Sun America. We got caught in a rotation and it was rotating out of it, and it was a really bad time. The fundamentals came through. We were holding at a time when no one wanted to hold. Then it doesn't matter what the fundamentals are, the stock is going down. From that standpoint, I'll time it, but if a group is not oversold, I'll just go in to it. I don't spend too much time timing it, I'll look at the chart, assuming it's gone up a lot, assuming it's not a heavily owned area. In other words: everyone is in the financials, and everyone wanted to get out when you and I wanted to play the fundamental trade on the earnings in Sun America. Everything worked out, except the rest of the market didn't want to be in it. That's an area I think is very important to concentrate on, it will be much more evident this year. You have these huge swings, like sector rotations. More and more I am going to be attuned to them to make sure we are getting the ball not only in a good fundamental story, and that technical indicators look good but that also that the sentimental Wall Street force, that group, doesn't have to be great, it just can't be bad. It can't be bad in overall or you will be dead, you can't fight that tide of rotation. That is what I am going to focus on this year as far as buying those stocks.

LIN: So you will have to be more discerning.

TOM: That's right.

LIN: I appreciate the time, Tom. I think we have had the time to explore some things that are, in general, different. It's interesting to hear someone who is a sales trading analyst talk about how they utilize information to generate money. We will be talking soon.

TOM: Thanks a lot.

Chapter 25

Robert Wibblesman

LIN:	Robert Wibblesman from Strome-Susskind and Company in Century City, right?
WIBBS:	Yeah.
LIN:	Bob, known as "Wibbs" and I have known each other for years, seems like twenty or so, and we both trained in the markets for most of our lives, I guess or all. What was your educational background?
WIBBS:	I was a Bachelor of Arts from Johns Hopkins.
LIN:	So, with a Liberal Arts degree, then what did you do?
WIBBS:	I got a job as a retail broker in a one office member firm in Baltimore.
LIN:	Then you went to Woods-Struthers at some point.
WIBBS:	Yes. In '68, '67 maybe.
LIN:	Then you have finished college around '60?
WIBBS:	'61.
LIN:	O.K., then we are of the same vintage, more or less. What has been your financial experience in terms of trading? What all have you traded?
WIBBS:	Well, I started out as a retail broker, and then as an institutional broker and my first experience actually trading or managing money really, came in the early

seventies   when I was with William O'Neal and ended up running the O'Neal Fund.

LIN: How many years were you with O'Neal?

WIBBS: I was there for three years.

LIN: O.K.

WIBBS: Only part of which was running the O'Neal Fund, and then I went to Kenner-Fitzgerald where I ended up being responsible for, or one of the ones responsible for, the position bids that we made, buy and sell side. Excuse me, long and short side. We would sit in the middle of the room and if one of the salesmen had a piece of merchandise to go and we thought that it was a group that was strong and therefore the customers for that day or the next day might be interested in that kind of merchandise, we would take it into inventory.

LIN: Speaking technically strong or fundamentally? What was your judgment?

WIBBS: Well, *my* judgment was based on whether I thought the stock was going to go up or not in case the customers were not interested in that. Generally, in an institutional trading area you have the situation where the, if institutions have generally been buying retail stocks, let's say, and you shop a piece of stock; somebody comes in to sell 50,000 May Company, let's say, and your buyers don't happen to want it at that moment based on they don't like the market or they think the stock is rich or whatever reason they don't respond, then a block trading firm has the option of either sending the seller away to try to have him sell it someplace else, or you might take the gamble and buy it into inventory and hope that the next day on the market....

LIN: Or do an agency, right?

WIBBS: No, this was in principle. You can do an agency, but you don't have a buyer, that's why this decision comes up.

LIN: I see.

WIBBS: If you don't have a buyer, or the ...let's just use a retail parallel. Let's just say that May Company is at forty dollars. All of a sudden some big institution comes in, and there *have* been buyers of retail stocks generally over the last few weeks, all of a sudden the seller comes in to sell 50,000 May at forty, and he is limited.

He will only sell at that forty, and you check around with the people who have been buying retail stocks and for whatever reason they don't want to buy May *or* they don't want to pay forty for it.

So, since (unintelligible) the only way you could do the business is if you got the other side. Meaning that the seller came in and you had to find a buyer or else you had to turn the seller away to go sell it on the floor of the Exchange or whatever.

So, to try to keep a merchandise flow, to try to satisfy the salesman who brought in that indication, very often we were called upon to say, "O.K., I will buy the 50,000 for the firm account at forty", and the way I would make that judgment would be based on whether I thought the stock was going to be O.K. at forty, and further it was a gamble that maybe the stock, if the stock went up to forty and a quarter or forty and a half the next day, that the customers may say "Humm, I did want that piece of stock after all" and they come in and buy it from you at forty or whatever price it is at the time.

So, I made the decision based on whether *I* thought it would be long groups or short stocks based on how I thought the groups were and based on how I thought that stock would perform.

LIN: O.K. That's it? O.K. So, did you ever trade commodities?

WIBBS: I have a seat on the New York Future's Exchange but I never used it. I trade commodities, you know, I trade

	S&P Futures and I've traded (unintelligible) futures in the past, and...
LIN:	You still (unintelligible) every now and then, don't you?
WIBBS:	Yeah, a lot. A lot.
LIN:	Daily?
WIBBS:	It's gotten to the point where it is fairly daily. It's part of our hedging process.
LIN:	O.K.
WIBBS:	Incidentally, in this interview, I really can't refer to much of Strom-Suskind in any terms of, you know, what we're up to.
LIN:	In other words, what the firm's style is or....?
WIBBS:	Yeah, I really can't do that. All I can do is really talk about me and even at that I have to get approval before I can be published because the FCC requires that people in the hedge fund business do not do anything that would smack of promoting themselves to attract money.
LIN:	Yeah, I understand, and yet there are a lot of interviews where people talk about what they do but not in a promotional standpoint. I guess....I mean, you tell me what you want to talk about and that way you can just drive what you are talking about. I think it would be interesting to hear the performance for last year. I mean, that's just a fact. That's not hearsay or....
WIBBS:	Yeah, but I think that if that goes into print that would be considered a form of....
LIN:	O.K.
WIBBS:	I'm just not sure, Lin. You see earnings, you see performance quoted in different newspapers and things like that and that's probably garnered by some reporter who gets a hold of one of the partners of the Fund and finds out what the number is.

LIN: Well, like that Forbes article that was done where you guys were quoted in there. What was wrong with....

WIBBS: But you see, the thing is if I'm in print saying something as a principal of Strom-Suskind-if I am in print saying something about it, it may be deemed to be promotional.

LIN: Oh, I see. I get it. In other words, if it's hearsay it doesn't matter, but if you're quoted then it does.

WIBBS: That's right.

LIN: O.K. I will have this thing, once it is typed, sent to you so that you can see whether there's parts you want to take out or whatever.

WIBBS: O.K.

LIN: O.K. Then, why don't we talk a little bit about what your style is and what you feel comfortable doing and how fully invested you feel comfortable being and sort of how you like the trade, what you like to do. What do you look for?

WIBBS: Now, are we talking about stocks or commodities?

LIN: Let's talk about stocks. Stocks is probably more straight forward and less gut.

WIBBS: Yeah, basically what I try to do is to be long at stocks that are emerging and I define emerging as a stock which has, after a period of doing nothing, it suddenly goes up faster than the market for three to six months, consolidates for a month or two and then breaks out.

I assume what happens in that process that the original past performance for the three to six months means that there's something unusual enough about the future of this company that people are willing to buy the stock under any market conditions and as consequence its relative performance goes up, because it goes up more than the market or because it down less severely than the market. And that sets up what I would deem to be over performance.

Then the next trick in getting a stock started is its ability to live through its first consolidation because usually in that performing the market for six months, a $30 stock may have gone to $45.

Or, it depends on the aspect of the market but generally, it goes up a lot. So, after stock goes up a lot and then begins to go sideways, it attracts profit taking and if during that period of consolidation of a couple months, it absorbs that profit taking and it then can move higher it's suggests to me that whoever wanted to sell it has sold it and its ready for another leg of better than market performance.

So, what I do, is I scan charts and look for pictures like that, the kind of pictures I've described and then I see whether that's in keeping with the rest of the group and similar groups because I believe in the market, in the broadest sense, there are three sub-sectors it's growth, income, or cyclical.

It's usually in a bull market, one of those three divisions of the sub sectors of the market is going up, one's going sideways, and ones going down, generally speaking.

So, if for an example, I see an emerging type picture and it happened to be in a growth stock and yet all of the market is being dominated by cyclical stocks, I may be less inclined to do that one.

Rather, I would probably try to look for a similar picture in the cyclical area because I want to be....

LIN: You want to be where the action is, right?

WIBBS: Yes. I want to be where the action is, but I don't want to be in the action to the point that it's very old business because what happens is that after the stock's been going up and performing better for the market for a couple years it inherently and structurally gets over bought and so the risk increases.

So, ideally the life cycle of a stock is such that it goes on for about two and a half years if everything works right, so if you give up the first six or eight months to identify the picture then you could figure the over performance could be a year to a year and a half and yet we see many stocks that have gone up for two years or two and a half years.

Everybody is talking about they're where the action is. Every time the market goes up two dollars this stock goes up four bucks, you know in that blow off stage. So that I want to be in the action but I want to try to be more in the emerging part of that excitement, rather than the more mature time of it.

Now the more mature time of it is easy for the short term trader because everyone is talking about it and everybody wants to own that stock. Lets take a recent example of a group that underwent a debacle. The telecommunications, last fall. They had been the hot stock for at least a year and in the Fall everything you read was that this was one of the (unintelligible) and yet stocks became over bought and when they rolled over a little, they went down thirty-five percent.

So when a stock is really in the far side of action central, yes it's easier because it seems to go up every day and you can buy every minor dip of a couple bucks and get away with it.

The problem is the risk is increasing unless you are a terrifically good seller, you take a chance of getting on the wrong side of that power curve and having pretty good mark down, and the obverse of all of this is true as well if you have a group which has been over performing and breaks down for the time is different so, in this case. if it breaks down for three months as opposed to going up for six months and goes sideways for four to five or six weeks and then breaks down again that usually is a sign that the thing is emerging, for sake of a better word, emerging on the down side and that becomes a short candidate.

So I'm very group oriented. I'm very oriented toward trying contain my interest to stocks and groups that are in what the broad category of stocks is doing well in the market.

LIN:	That all makes sense. O.K. So your style basically is to ferret out which groups are going to perform better than the market and then along with that you make a call to how you feel about the market so if the market is going down, you don't want to be heavily in one group that just happens to be the only group around. People will hit that at the end of the line when they cash everything out.
WIBBS:	Well yeah, if you go from a minor sell off in a market to an intermediate sell off, during the end of the intermediate sell off you will have a period of usually some number of days where the market perversely preys on strength. So the strong stocks become source of funds because they are the only ones that people can sell.
LIN:	Yeah.
WIBBS:	And then as fear broadens, as we're seeing now......
LIN:	O.K. So we were taking about how perversely they take the good girls of the bad girls at the end of a line.
WIBBS:	Right. At the end of the sell off , a lot of times even the ugly ones don't go down they just go after the pretty ones at the very end they went for the pretty ones and we are seeing apparently on March 29th.

That now where semi-conductors had been the absolute strength of the market for the last month and a half and now the last few days they have just gotten cratered and we are seeing other strong stocks, high relative strength stocks, just getting hammered.

So that's what happens late in the sell off and the market has been topped out for say a month and a half now and it's finally getting to what had been the strongest stocks.

LIN:	The autos got cratered the last few days and today.
WIBBS:	Actually yesterday the autos bounced a little bit. I don't know how they acted today.
LIN:	Well Chrysler off a couple. I think two and a quarter.

Can you talk about how you performed over the last three years.

WIBBS: I really shouldn't.

LIN: O.K. Can you talk about....You're a partner, a general partner?

WIBBS: Yes.

LIN: Co-general partner in Strom-Suskind, which is a partnership that goes long and short and trades futures and overseas?

WIBBS: Yes.

LIN: Securities?

WIBBS: Yes.

LIN: O.K. What has helped you in the last year and what has hurt you?

WIBBS: What has helped me is my style. What has hurt me are two things....

LIN: Your style, and what else?

WIBBS: Very often in the inactivity or the unwillingness to broaden my line and bet myself as big as I should, to do what I should do, with consistency. I'll see a picture, it's an attractive picture and the market will be questionable and I don't do the stock because I don't trust the market.

Often the market will go down as I think and yet the stock that I wanted to buy doesn't go down, it goes up. So I let market judgment interfere with individual stock selection. That is one of the more chronic problems I've had.

LIN: So that, like today you really feel like, okay the market is tanking and I see some stocks that I like. I like the technical pattern but you don't point them because you're afraid that the market might collapse again tomorrow?

WIBBS: Right but this is not a good time to make that comment because now we have a throw away market. I'm speaking about more when the market's modestly an over bought territory and I think it might roll over and then it rolls over for three or four days and it's just a short term correction and all of a sudden the stock I didn't buy goes up a lot.

When we get the throw away of the high relative strength stocks, I just shut down.

LIN: In other words, you don't want to play because you don't want to get hurt.

WIBBS: That's right. So I just stop completely

LIN: So you go defensive.

WIBBS: Yeah. I don't regret that.

LIN: Unless we are seeing a major top in formation, it's tough to play it when you get far...When your momentum gets going too much to the downside, it's too late to play it?

WIBBS: No. Then the trick is to use the other logic about short selling, but one of the things I've noticed in the last three years that's been a problem is that the thing I originally described as how to pick the shorts has been very spotty because we have really been, overall, in a Bull market.

You can tell in the numbers of all the short sellers how unsuccessful shorting has been. I've noticed in the last two or three years that the only real short leverage comes from shorting the leaders as they curl down after being...getting to the top of their own channels, and since I like leaders, it's hard for me to shorten them.

So, the two things that I think have been restrictive to me have been; number one, one of the things that hampers me, let's say, is letting market judgment keep me away from what I should be doing on stock judgment. I'm right enough about the market to have some measure of respect for it, but often it is just an inhibiting factor where I should just do the stocks, fully do the stocks.

LIN: And forget the market?

WIBBS: Forget the market and use the normal escape parameters I use for getting out stocks, and run the stock position in the absence of a market judgment.

LIN: That's hard to do as you say.

WIBBS: Very difficult to do for one thing. Now....

LIN: In the middle of the market, there is one particular stock and yet all around you there are crashes going on and you just.... So you miss that move which you should have been in because of the market judgment.

WIBBS: Yeah. So it's tough and it's something that you have to deal with. The other thing that hampers me a lot is I end up, not out of design, but just out of a sense of caution under investing.

WIBBS: Me too.

(Wibbs asks to take a break from the interview here. Interview is resumed as follows.)

LIN: O.K., here we go.

WIBBS: Anyway, I've forgotten where we left off....

LIN: We were talking about how you use your general market to correlate the market and the stocks and how that can confuse the issue, because you might have great selections but somehow your fear of loss because of the market keeps you from jumping on the ones that look great to you.

WIBBS: Right. I guess if you could say as a personality profile my fear of loss is greater than my fear of victory.

LIN: Well, that's interesting. You've never seemed particularly like you were an optimist or a pessimist, but when you see people lose money like in 1987, it's got to have some impact for the rest of your life.

WIBBS: Yes.

LIN: I think that's part of what happens with people that are pros is that after they've gone through a real bad time. They trade, they make money and they're solid in their performance, but they never go crazy because they know they can be taken out and they have a lot of respect for the market.

WIBBS: Yeah.

LIN: I guess one last question. How do you set up mentally to do that having been with buy side houses?

WIBBS: The short side?

LIN: Yeah.

WIBBS: I'd say, buy side houses by and large, their analysts don't know how to make money.

LIN: So....

WIBBS: Excuse me, it's the sell side.

LIN: Well, I'm sorry. I got you...

WIBBS: Theoretically as a broker, you're supposed to be Little Mary Sunshine pumping out the firm's product.

LIN: Buy, buy, buy.

WIBBS: One of the things, in *none* of those capacities as a broker, was I ever willing to embrace that philosophy and just be on the phone and my gross will prove it. (Laughs) I was more interested in being right than rich.

LIN: Yeah.

WIBBS: As a consequence I didn't just go out and pound on the customers to buy the firm's product line. I was really trying to sell me more than anything because my long-term inclination, or interest rather, was to end up in a money management role and I think while there are *plenty* of successful Pollyanna money managers, I just felt a certain cynicism was very, very vital in staying alive.

LIN: O.K., and keeping the customers alive, I guess.

WIBBS: Yeah. Absolutely. Absolutely.

LIN: O.K. We've pretty much covered the bases and have an ability now to kind of look at your profile and sort of match it up with how you think and how your style is and that will be kind of interesting.

WIBBS: As for performance, all I can refer to is certain things that are ancient history. When I was running the O'Neal Fund, in an eight month period I took the Fund from number two-ninety-two in its category up to number twenty-two in a difficult market in 1973. While I was a (unintelligible) I was running some partner's money and, by and large, came in somewhere around twenty percent a year, something like that. I guess my performance goal is I hope for a minimum of twenty percent a year

LIN: Have you been able to pretty much consistently able to attain that?

WIBBS: Well, up until Strom-Suskind, I can't comment on any performance for Strom-Suskind, but yeah, it's been pretty consistent and it ends up under optimizing myself, but nonetheless comes into the good numbers.

LIN: O.K..

WIBBS: And I'm working to *improve* that number by trying to force myself to be more invested.

LIN: Well, it sounds like you've got your rest of the year resolution right in hand.

WIBBS: Yes. Incidentally, if this *does* get published, you were asking about limitations...there were a couple of stocks that got away from me on the down side where I didn't sell them fast enough last year, so my Christmas resolution this year take no prisoners and so far I've been doing that and I feel much more comfortable with that. It's *amazing* how easy it is, no matter *how* sophisticated you are, to get trapped in stocks. It is just *astonishing.*

LIN: It is astonishing to me too. I mean, I'm looking at one now that I got a point in, and it's an eight dollar stock, and I'm justifying it because I think I know something that other people don't know.

WIBBS: *Whatever* your style is, there are occasions where you actually *believe* in a stock and you think it's being carried down by market reasons. Another trap is that, particularly in a bull market, you see stocks break for a short while, scare you out, and then *immediately* reverse and run back up.

So what happens is you're getting a more mature market. You get tired of selling and being wrong. So, occasionally you slip into the trap that when the market curls, and it's serious on the down side, that you don't want to sell the fourteenth one wrong for that period of time and you decide to hold one for a little bit thinking "Well, it's going to bounce and I *really* like this one" and the next thing you know you have a big loss on your hands and it happens no matter how sophisticated you are.

Occasionally you get "Red Dogged", so this year I've really tried to work on that and make sure that no matter how repulsive it is for me to sell something. I mean today, for example, I cut down coming into today where I was minimally exposed...

LIN: I've clipped some stuff off today that hurt, but I look back and it was so smart.

WIBBS: Yeah, well that's what's happened to me the last three days I've been selling stuff some of which hurt and it turned out...I thought I made a bad sale yesterday in one stock and it turns out today it's broken seven-eighths on a sixteen dollar base which was a big percentage.

So today, I still have some positions in which I believe, but I just closed my eyes and cut half of them.

So my exposure is even further reduced and so when we talk about limiting things, as professional as I view myself and as much of a pro, a vet, as I am, last year I had a couple of stocks that just *burned* me.

LIN: What do you try and keep your losses down to?

WIBBS: I have no hard and fast rules. Obviously, ten percent would be a standard line, but I find that I try to stop stocks based on minor things that they have done. For example, if you have a two or three day pullback in the market and/or stock, whatever level it achieves on the down side, wherever it stopped going down, I use that as a stop/loss. Now, that may be at a loss for *me*, or it may be at a reduced profit for me.

So if I buy a stock at forty and immediately after I buy it, the market rolls over and the stock bottoms out at thirty-eight and a half and the stock moves up again, thirty-eight and a half is my stop.

If I buy it at forty and it goes up to forty-five, and then it pulls back to forty-three and a half, moves up and takes a swing at forty-five and doesn't make it and rolls over, then forty-three and a half is my new stop.

So I don't do any program, sort of moving stops or automatic stops or anything like that, but I take the most recent pullback point as my reference point for a stop/loss. So, if I bought a stock at forty and its recent pullback reference point was thirty-eight, well then I adopt that as the stop/loss going in and then adjust for upward or downward. Adjust is upward, excuse me, from there.

LIN: I gotcha. So, that's paramount as a consideration of your trading plan, sounds like.

WIBBS: You know, if somebody reads the book "Market Wizards", outside of Jimmy Roger's comments where he was never wrong, I certainly wouldn't want that to be published. Where he admitted that he was never wrong. Every other guy, the *foremost* consideration is damage control, damage control, damage control.

LIN: It's what kills ya. It's really what kills us.

WIBBS: Yeah.

LIN: You know, it's funny cause I really haven't admitted it to myself personally, but I guess that's what I'm looking at this year too, because I've noticed I kind of went out of trading gear about two weeks ago and I couldn't figure out why. It's because I wasn't making money. So, then all of a sudden if I wasn't making money then I had to stop losing money because the things I was in weren't going up any more.

WIBBS: Well, I always find that....

LIN: That's why I put the interview off the other day, is that I was thinking I'm getting hurt here and I don't understand it.

Chapter 26

Larry Williams with John Furey

LIN: Larry, could you tell me a little bit about your educational background? How did you manage to get involved with the financial markets?

LARRY: I was not a good student at all in high school. I started college playing football at B.Y.U., went on a football scholarship and my major was Art, and I quickly realized I wasn't a great football player and my art work was not as good as the other people in school. So I switched to Journalism and enjoyed that because I was interested in writing and maybe being a copywriter or working in an advertising agency; looked like there was a lot of money in that business, and did that, completed with a degree from the University of Oregon School of Journalism and worked for J. Walter Thompson, the world's largest advertising agency in New York City. But I was real frustrated in that, because I was young and probably thought I was better than I really was and I wanted to do a lot of things, and someplace along the line somebody pointed out to me in the newspaper some stock was up a point and I had no idea what that was, what it meant, and I said "What does that mean?" and the guy said

"Well, it means that you could have made a hundred dollars if you would have bought a hundred shares of that stock yesterday" and I went "Wow!". This is the mid-sixties, and a hundred bucks was a lot of money, and I thought "This is for me! This-is-for-me!". How do you figure out if it goes up a point or not, it looked pretty easy, you know, cause the previous day I also noticed a stock had been up a point, so I thought that was all you gotta do. If it goes up one damn point, you buy it and if it goes up the next damn point... WRONG! (Laughs) Real wrong. It was like, you know, Old Man Green just tapped me on the shoulder and my life has been different ever since; but the journalism background was good because it really teaches you about interviewing and research and doing your homework and I was blessed, I had a professor, a guy named Max Wales, who really taught us to use libraries. Of course, I guess now, if he was teaching, it would be how to use a computer, but it was how to access data and how to think. He was really very helpful in letting us come up with our own solutions to problems he would present us, and then *he* would give solutions from *his* own experience and his solutions were always, let's say off-the-wall, very unique solutions so he taught us to think differently and that combined with Art, I think, has helped me a lot in the Markets because I look at charts a lot, and I suspect I can see relationships and things that the average person doesn't see because I just, I mean, I'm used to looking, I mean if you are going to draw something then you have to really look to see what's going on there; the shading, the colors, the lines, the textures, and there are things in charts that I see and say "Look at that" and people say

"Ah, I never saw that before". That, combined with the kind of the hard core, the statistical approach, if you will, of journalism, of getting your facts, I think was very helpful to me.

LIN: When you are looking at a chart, say you are looking at the S&P, do you ever think of it in terms of it telling a story; shake out, blow off, volume patterns, past story, and present pattern and anything as it relates to the future?

LARRY: Not much, no. If I am looking at a chart, I am looking for relationships. If there's a "story", it would be the story of "What is the public...what have they just done and what will they most likely do" on the assumption that most likely they will be wrong. So, if the Market has a *huge* move in a direction up or down, that is probably the public and the public habitually does things at the wrong *time*. Not necessarily...they might do the right thing at this price level, but in terms of timing, their timing is way off. So, I'm real interested in looking at what *time* I think they are doing something and what they are thinking. Are they thinking "Hah, I'm getting out of this market and throw everything up" or are they going to say "I've got to buy." They've just been pushed so much they've got to get in and buy, which is probably the time to sell. I think of it in terms of that. But I've heard some people, at least after talking to Gary Anderson, I think was his name, who had these great dialogues. He would compare the markets to horses running in the wind or something, and I could never get it that far. I don't see it as an on-going story. I see it as little bits and pieces; the market is set up to do something now, and I remember I saw the market in this exact same pattern a while ago, or a long time ago, and I can go into the computer and check and see if my memory is correct or not.

LIN: Which leads me to one of the things that you are well-known for, which is pattern recognition. How do you interpret things based on facts? How do you interpret charts based on facts?

LARRY: The easiest way to do it for me is to identify the pattern, the general pattern the market is in. Let's say, yesterday in the market, we had an inside day and we had a up-close the day before, and that up-close day had a lower high and a lower low. I can then go into the computer and say "O.K., this has occurred in the past: an inside day with a down close which is preceded by a lower high, lower low, but with a higher close. What's happened in the next couple of days?

LIN: So this is your probability analysis?

LARRY: Right. So there I have to get subjective, and I think this is probably an interesting day, my mind says "Yeah, this will probably be a buy, if I recall" so then I can go in and specifically ask the computer from past data what happens, given my general buy rule and my general exit rule, and then I can see if in fact it is a bullish pattern or a bearish pattern. Sometimes I'm surprised, but most of the time I know most of these patterns so well that I know if it's a buy pattern or a sell pattern. Occasionally though, I'll be surprised and according to the data it's bullish and I was bearish and so then I will trade accordingly.

LIN: Do you have any particular preference as to what markets you trade?

LARRY: My preference is the bond market, the S&P's. If I was pushed to trade in another market, it would be coffee.

LIN: And *why* do you like those markets?

LARRY: I like the bonds and S&P markets because of the quality of the players in the market. These are not nickel-and-dime guys trading S&P's at a margin of $11,000.00. These are real players. They're not skittish. They don't get as frightened as quickly as a guy whose got $600.00 margin up. Also, there's a lot more known about the S&P's. This is an average of 500 stocks, therefore trades are less erratic, less hectic than say, coffee, or pork bellies, or hogs.

LIN: It's a thicker market.

LARRY: It's a thicker market and because of that we got more data on it. We know there's something that influences stock prices, absolutely. Interest rates, inflation, bond market; it has some very dominant time periods when it rallies and when it declines. So, it's a very well-known market if you have done your research, there's a lot there. It has a definite trading characteristic to it, and it can't be influenced, because it represents 500 stocks, as quickly by a bit of news as say, pork bellies, can be. The Bond market I like that because, again, it's a commercial market, the primary players are banks and institutions and it is a broad market. You can get in and you can get out. You don't have any liquidity problems to speak of. It's a broader market and it also has some real strong characteristics that I feel I have uncovered. The reason for trading coffee is simply that it is really volatile, and that is the same reason for trading pork bellies. Of course, I've been trading pork bellies for so long that I have a little sense of what they are doing, but if you are going to make money, you gotta be involved in the markets. Most people want to trade oats or corn or something that doesn't move, and you know, nothing risked, nothing gained.

LIN: I've got John Fury here with me from Scottsdale, Arizona whose company is Humanagement and who led me to get involved with him in writing a book and I wanted to bring John into this discussion because John has taken Larry's personal options profile and knows quite a bit about how Larry thinks, and what his volition is. John, do you have any questions you would like to ask Larry?

JOHN: Yeah, about three hundred. Remember as you were going through college, and you had the benefit of a very good professor in your Journalism class? When you first came across this thing, this stock market, and you saw that if it went up you could make money and if it went down you lost money and therefore there must be some simplish rules. What was it in your mind or in your gut that propelled you forward, given that you are someone who very much, from an instinctive point of view, looks forward and sees opportunity and then gathers information afterwards. What makes you have it, can you remember? Cause I know it was some time ago.

LARRY: I think it was just that looked like it was easy money. It looked like, "Gee, I would be able to make money doing this." And then something triggered my mind, "Oh, yeah, I heard people made a lot of money trading stocks or buying stocks." And it just looked like easy   the outside looking in.

JOHN: What money. From we do, what we put our energy in to, is to do things that allow us to buy at an ever better level, to succeed at an ever better level. At that point in your life, did you need to make money?

LARRY: Oh, sure. I didn't have any, I had zero money.

JOHN: All right. So this was "I've got to make it somehow, I really want to make it, I'm hungry to make it, and here looks like the easiest way to do that." Was that the kind of what was going on?

LARRY: Yeah. It looked like, I mean I realized I had some writing abilities, some promotional and marketing abilities, but that didn't have the excitement of trading, and there wasn't the sense that you could make as much money as quickly. That to be a good writer, it might be a career of twenty or thirty years, but you get one bull market and you've made a lot of money. So, I think there was some sense of timing to it, John, that it was there to be had. And I think that I, wrongly at the time, felt that maybe this had to do with luck, trading in the markets, and that I had a degree of luck, and that would always be my, one of my, calling cards.

JOHN: To what degree did the risk inherent in the market place, and I guess I should ask, did you understand it was a risky thing to do in the first place? I mean, you could lose everything you put in there very easily.

LARRY: I have never in my life, then or now, have comprehended risk. Risk, I don't think has ever been a concern.

JOHN: It hasn't been a concern.

LARRY: Never been a concern.

JOHN: But you knew it was there, you mean you just didn't worry about it?

LARRY: I mean I never even knew it was there, maybe that is why it has never been a concern. I mean, I just always figure that, like I'm a rubber ball, I'm just going to bounce, and it doesn't matter, things will take care of themselves. God will provide in one form or another.

JOHN: So, if I may, you stated in fact that risk does not worry you.

LARRY: No.

JOHN: You're very comfortable with that?

LARRY: Yeah. I hear all these people and they have all these considerations about the market and stuff and risk has really never been...I mean I don't want to lose money, but it's never been a concern. I know it probably should be, but it never has been very much of a concern.

JOHN: Once you got into trading and you started to learn the ropes and how this works and what all the inside buzz words were and everything else, at what point did you find that acquiring a lot of data and having information, accurate information, was going to be a very important component to your success?

LARRY: Oh, probably within the first three months of following the market I realized that numbers were involved, statistics were involved, therefore there was data you could examine, and I read a book by a guy named Gil Haller. It really excited me because this guy has done some research, and he had presented his conclusions, and I was fortunate enough to get to meet Gil, and to spend some time with him, and get a sense of "Oh, yeah, maybe you can predict the future based on the past." That if you can study this stuff, and maybe get a conclusion on what will take place in the future.

JOHN: If you hadn't met Gil Haller, and you hadn't gotten this insight that we can predict the future from the past, do you think it would have changed your trading style? Do you think you may have gone a different direction?

LARRY: It's hard to say. I don't think so, though, I think my, the way I think my mind operates, is , I do want to know, I do want to get information. I've always been a student of *things*. When I was in college, I didn't have particularly great grades and I was kind of a goof off type of guy, not maybe, not wild is the right word, but I wasn't known as a great student, yet I won the library contest for having the best library on a subject matter which surprised the heck out of all of my fraternity brothers and all my friends, that I would have a library that was a massive library. I have just always been into books, I've always loved books and books of course, give you references which you can study and read and maybe learn about what to do. So, to that extent, I have always been a person who has likes to read; to arrive at some sort of operating rules.

JOHN: Were you introduced to books as a child?

LARRY: Oh, yeah. I was a heavy art reader. As far back as I can remember.

JOHN: And was this motivation something that your father or your mother had shown you or a teacher, I mean......?

LARRY: Oh, yeah, I'm certain that there was something......of course, you know, unfortunately I was born before television, almost before radio, before transistor radio at least, and it was certainly an escape to be able to get beyond a little boy in a little town out in the West and I could get places by reading books and I got to those places and saw that the world was a whole lot bigger than what I think my friends saw the world as being.

JOHN: Would you say you tend to avoid physical or manual tasks in life?

LARRY: That's a conflict. I've always been involved in athletics. It's been a dialogue conflict with myself. I was all-state football. I lettered in track, cross-country, wrestling, football. That was the athletic side of me. I was never a great athlete but it was always a contradiction because all of my athletic friends got very poor grades so I naturally got poor grades too, because I didn't want to be different from them, and at the same time I loved to do some of the academic or intellectual things. At that point it wasn't cool to be both; if you were one you were one, you weren't the other. It was easier to be more physical at that point and eventually in my life I got to the point where I realized that my physical body wasn't enough to make a career out of and it was O.K. to use my mind. In a way, I thought I was dumb as a kid too. I had an older brother who was a brilliant, brilliant guy and I wasn't as smart as him and I could see that and so I thought I was dumb. Eventually I got a reckoning that maybe I wasn't dumb; I wasn't brilliant but I did have some intelligence that I could use.

JOHN: Do you think that the challenge of the sports, and then later the challenge of mastering your intellectual capacity; when I use the word challenge as the key word I am trying to look at, is that something that feels right in terms of the way you have approached life, that it has been a challenge and you have risen to that occasion?

LARRY: Yeah, I like the challenges but you know, it's an interesting question because I think earlier on, in athletics, I did it for acceptance. I played football to be accepted by my friends and so the girls would say "Oh, yeah, he wears a leather jacket", and they would dance with you. I think the athletics, created total acceptance and I've just had that cognition now, . Later on, I got into the challenges of life. Which I now thoroughly get off on; the challenge of the market, the challenge of running marathons, the challenge of playing handball at a competitive level. Those challenges really excite me, but initially that wasn't the reason for the athletics.

JOHN: So would it be fair to say that the impressions that you create to people outside of yourself, and therefore how you define yourself, was, from what you were saying just now about your earlier life and how you were accepted by people, and now, which is rather different, cause now you are accepted, now were those impressions really important at that point?

LARRY: I'm not certain I understand the question.

JOHN: O.K., let me put it like this. The INVENT instincts which are dominant have two very strong characteristics. One of those characteristics is that we do things, to a very large degree, for the impression of whom we are that it creates. One of the reasons we do this is because, unlike the ORDER instinct, or the SEEK instinct, the ORDER being the present tense instinct and the SEEK being the past tense instinct, the INVENT instinct is so future oriented, that we very rarely leave a mark of our existence on the fabric of society around us. So, because we don't have a mark, such as the writing of a book, which is a SEEK thing to do, which is your second suit, leaves a tangible physical product for someone after our death to pick up and say "Oh, this is what Larry Williams contributed to the world". The ORDER instinct would organize instructions, create institutions. The INVENT is so future oriented, so visionary, speculative, probability oriented, that they really don't make anything, leave anything that is left behind as a tangible representation of their passing. So, what they attempt to do is to need, in order to build their sense of self, they tend to need recognition from people right there and then, because there will never be, in their minds, and this is a pure INVENT instinct, there will never be a monument to their having been there. Does that make sense?

LARRY: Yeah.

JOHN: Now, your seek instinct, which is your second dominant, definitely is the writing, the researching, and collecting of data and stuff. But from what you were saying, getting an acceptance was important earlier in life, which is one of the marks of the invent. The second mark of the invent is taking on life as a challenge. In other words, when we stop worrying about the people outside of us, and what they think of us, then we start to turn to what is needed, and the invent need is to have a challenge in life. I mean, the worst thing in the world for an invent person is not to have a challenge. They basically atrophy, they stagnate. So, for you, I'm trying to see if the invent instinct was always dominant, it was always dominant, but rather it manifest itself as dominant throughout your life. So, it was almost a transition between the playing of sports because that was what got you accepted and what got people admiring you and then you moved through that phase into the next phase, which was your life's challenge and you had to go out and make it.

LARRY: Yeah.....I'm there. Part of the accept thing, I guess, was to be funny. I could kind of be the class clown in a way and that was maybe in college. I could be the wild guy to come up with the wildest, craziest things to do; to jump off bridges, or do whatever it was, to do some great practical joke, and that got acceptance. But there was always, I mean, even now I can't believe I did the things I did for practical joke humor. Talk about invent, they were really far out things.

LIN: Oh really.

LARRY: Oh, wow. Let me tell ya.

LIN: Give a couple of examples, if you would.

LARRY: Well, a quick one would be climbing up the back of a drive-in movie screen a hundred feet in the air and tossing a dummy over so it would look like the guy hung himself in front of everybody in the movie theater, to dressing up like monks from another planet and going after some psycho-babble type people and shucking and jiving them that another guy and I were the messengers that they had been waiting for and keeping that guise going for a couple of weeks in Eugene, Oregon with these people.

LIN: Really!

LARRY: Oh, yeah. It was really something. Well, this guy was a hypnotist and he charged my fraternity brothers, we thought, too much money and so we were going to get even with him in some fashion, so we did this incredible scam type of thing where he really thought we were from another planet. We dressed up with weird clothes and weird colors, and everything and kept this thing going and they had thirty people coming out to see us in the evening for our prophesies. We were just college kids.

JOHN: You had a political vision didn't you. The vision that you had and the solutions that you had for the problem, places and people around you, and they didn't get it and they were more interested in the big picture not the steps along the way.. Since then you said, really it sounded you were disappointed in the lack of ability of the people to see a better way for the future, that you have detached yourself from the political system.

LARRY: Right, I won the primary overwhelmingly—biggest margin in the history of the State of Montana—because the people in the primaries are your party members. You have some allegiance there and a primary is usually devoted to get out party people and they can relate with the issues. But then when you try to go out and get in everybody, not only the other side of the aisle but people that are apolitical, that is where it fell on deaf ears. That was very, very frustrating. So I said, hey, they don't get it, I'm out of the system. I don't care. The world is going to go to hell or whatever it is going to do and I'm not going to be part of it. I'm not going to waste my time on it.

JOHN: At that point in your life, do you remember, with the large amounts of your psyche and energy that you were putting into life, were you willing to give it to a cause outside of yourself? And then after that was there a shift that said...

LARRY: Oh yes, clearly. My whole existence for two senatorial campaigns was about what we could do to make Montana better or what we could do to improve the political process and get economic growth in America. And when in my case it didn't work out—I wasn't elected—I just walked away from it. I admire—I've got some friends that are still in politics and they have won some elections and helped my positions and they keep working so that maybe they can keep the faith. But I... You know... Now I'm going to get back into making money which got me to the point I could run for the senate, *threw(?)* a lot of money on it, and said O.K. fine money is the issue and I'll get back to making money and if I want to do something altruistically I'll donate some money to something.

LIN: It is interesting, you're take on money and your revitalized efforts in pursuit of it and there is a common thread that runs between us in terms of an association we had with Craig McFarland who's very existence was to get money at all cost without concern for people who got trampled in the process. There is such a simple difference between people who see money in a good light and others who see it as a means to an end and ultimately destroy themselves and others in the process in the pursuit of money.

LARRY: Yet in Craig's case—I think with Craig it was not only the pursuit of money but, you know what, Lin? He had to beat you even if it wasn't money. He had to better you. That was my sense about Craig. He always had...

LIN: Evil instinct...

LARRY: Oh yeah. He had to beat people down to be happy. If he couldn't beat you down he wasn't happy. We were playing handball one time at the Pacheco Club in Monterey. I happen to be a little better handball player than Craig so I'm beating him pretty thoroughly and so he decided we are going to play a different way—with racquets with a handball instead. Which is kind of like racquet ball except a hand ball is real hard and he hit this thing right into my back. I had a huge, big blood blister on my back where I got hit. Then, of course, Craig was through, we didn't have to play anymore. And that, boy...

LIN: That ended the game?

LARRY: But Craig had to make it, he had to definitely make it so that you would lose and then he could be really happy. Then you could be his friend too. If he could beat you...if he decimated you so much the better.

LIN: He had to be top dog.

LARRY: Yeah, he had a lot of low energy friends that he could control because they knew he was more powerful than them. Guys like Lin and I, I think, were a little frightening to him because we didn't roll under.

LIN: Right, right...we could catch him in the act.

LARRY: ...and we'd catch him, "Wait a minute, what are you trying to do..."

LIN: He was the guy the FBI caught in Monaco, he'd had plastic surgery, he put on a lot of weight—like 30 pounds—

LARRY: And embezzled 51 million dollars or something like that? Was that the number?

LIN: He kept 2 sets of books. One for reality, one for the banker and one for the IRS. Three set of books: Reality, the IRS and the bankers. And the bankers got inflated numbers, the IRS got deflated numbers, and reality was somewhere else. He lied to the bankers and then took off with the money that he borrowed from the bank based on inflated real estate.

LARRY: Leaving his wife and child behind.

JOHN: Good God.

LARRY: To deal with all the...

LIN: Barbara was a gorgeous and wonderful lady.

JOHN: That's incredible. One last question then and then we will move back to your question. To what degree in your life is there a consciousness about the fact that you have the basic intuitive impulse into the ____ and way you should be putting your energy and what you should be doing and what would work, not just in your trading, but also in the other products and the other books that you have written? To what degree is there a consciousness about the fact that intuitive impulse is followed up by research because it makes impulse feel more comfortable to you?

LARRY: How do I tie together impulse and research?

JOHN: Well, it is not how do you tie them together because as when you and I spoke before, clearly you get a gut feel for something and say, "I know this is going to win." And then what you do is do research and a enormous amount of information that supports that initial conclusion. My question is, how conscious is that? In other words is something you really think about?

LARRY: Oh yeah. Very much so.

JOHN: O.K. And if you didn't or couldn't do the research to back up the initial gut intuition, would you still go with the *gut intuition (?)* ?

LARRY: I wouldn't play.

JOHN: You wouldn't play. O.K. That's important. Would that go for both the trading and other products or would it be more specific to your trading because you know that it's so...

LARRY: If the stakes were of any consequence, if the stakes were inconsequential I'll go with my ego and say I know better than you... But if there are any consequence to the stakes, I want to make certain that I thoroughly know the subject matter. One of the things my dad always taught me was that if you are going to speak in public, you have to have earned the right to speak in public. And what I picked up on that is if you are going to trade the market or do something you better have earned the right to do it and that doesn't come by just having some egotistical viewpoint or theoretical viewpoint. It comes from, in my case I guess, from doing the research, knowing the subject matter so that I can talk about it. Or not just talk but trade it or do it or whatever it is. Talking *isn't* the same as doing it in this case.

JOHN: Quite right. You're not going to have an opinion unless you've done your homework.

LARRY: Absolutely. People call me up all the time and say, "What do you think of this market?" I say, "I don't have any idea." They say, "Well you're supposed to be the expert." I say, "I don't trade it, I don't follow it, I don't know." I'm not the guy for that question. I don't want to commit to something unless I really do know it.

JOHN: Do you often get into brainstorming sessions with people?

LARRY: No.

JOHN: Do you not enjoy brainstorming and sort of bouncing ideas and solutions...?

LARRY: I don't have any brains to brainstorm with. I have one guy that I will do some stuff with Tommy Marks, but...no friends.

LIN: It seems like you used to do brainstorming with Justin. Remember Justin?

LARRY: Justin Stone.

LIN: Yeah. When we were next-door neighbors in Carmel Valley in 1968.

LARRY: Yeah, but you know what I learned? Lin, when we were younger, I think that out of fear we went to older people and tried to get their ideas and stuff and at some point I said to myself, "These guys don't know." Justin was to me kind of a...

LIN: He was a weirdo.

LARRY: A weirdo con man guy—con man is too strong of a word—but highly opinionated and I gravitate toward highly opinionated people: They have the answers therefore I don't have to do my research; I can just side step everything and collect the $200 and go. And at some point I finally realized, wait, these guys don't know any more than I do and I better do my work myself. But yes, I would go to anybody to listen to them to see what they had to say about any subject matter. Now I don't have a real good discriminating mode of operating but a little better than it used to be. I've seen a bunch of wacky people out there with wacky ideas about everything from the market to whatever.

JOHN: You have referred several times to your father and the things your father taught you. Would you say you developed very strong values as a child that were given to you and that you've kept and adhered to?

LARRY: Well, I was given strong values, I didn't attach to them early on. I came back to them. I realized that was right.

JOHN: So it took you an exploration to discover that the values you were given really had value, there was a reason for them.

LARRY: Yeah, finally I realized that the world does work a little easier this way than that way.

LIN: You strived all your life that I know of in the business world to be right. In other words, to be right is to make money. To be wrong is to lose money. And yet with these things you're testing you're very much like me. You're very low in order when it has to do with following rules and being disciplined. You're more of a creative person than you are a disciplined person, which is the same as myself. O.K. So you spent a lot of your time researching and trying to figure out how to be right and making money. Do you think you have gone as far as you want to go in that direction? Or will you always spend time trying to find, you know, the secret..."Heavenly Grail"?

LARRY: In my ideal world someone would hire me and put me in a little corner with a computer loaded with data and say, "Here you give us stuff and we will go follow it and trade it." I realize my weaknesses are the trading aspect of it. I've got students that trade a lot better than I do. The trading allows me to *do* the research. And it totally isn't all that other stuff as well, but in my ideal world I would be doing nothing but grinding out research and knowing about the market and doing it even if there wasn't money involved—just the challenge part of it.

JOHN: So the challenge backed up by the...

LARRY: *The challenge is a good thing* and fortunately *beating it* means you get money in this business. But I know that is clearly not my strength. I am not a very good trader. It is hard for me to do all the things you're supposed to do as well. But, boy, when it comes to researching, that is where I get really turned on.

LIN: Another question really that has to do with research that I was going to ask you earlier was, I've been told everybody can be right and wrong—it just depends on the time frame. And that there are minute-to-minute traders who will go for 1/8th of a point or whatever the lowest denomination of the trade is, *scalpers (?)*. There are day traders, there are overnight traders who are in it today and out of it tomorrow, week traders, position

	traders, and so on. What have you found is the ideal time to hold things that are commodities.
LARRY:	I think it depends on ones basic nature. It is real important to know what your basic timing nature is because if you're a long-term player and you try to short-term trade you'll go crazy or, even worse yet; real insanity comes if you're a short-term trader trying to hold for the long term because you gyrate up and down. In my case I like to get into a trade today and out within 3 days. That fits my temperament pretty well, I like that.
LIN:	I think it suits your subscribers, it seems like, who like the action, they want to make money...
LARRY:	They want some action; they would probably like to be 6 to 12 days, maybe 16 days. Then there's the other group who would like to be in and out 10 times during the day who I don't even want to be involved with. I don't know how to do it; it's too active for me. I think the average person probably would like to be a 6 to 10 day ho
JOHN:	You probably wouldn't describe a 2 to 3 day trading window as a chaotic one at all.
LARRY:	Not at all.
JOHN:	And, yet, there are other probably like Peter Lynch who would say that is real chaotic.
LARRY:	Right.
JOHN:	You know, let's talk 3 to 6 months here because that's more a...
LARRY:	But you see I'm more impatient than he is. And I think that comes because I started poor and I've got to make money today or how am I going to stay alive? But if you've got a big bankroll, then you can say, "Well, O.K., we'll see what happens here in 3 or 4 or 5 months." But

if you come from the position of having nothing in your life at all, no money in your family or in your early existence at all, you need to make money now, today, quickly.

JOHN: But now you have money but still you trade the same way.

LARRY: Yeah, because that's me that's what I've learned.

JOHN: You see, and I'm wondering if that's something you've learned or whether that's touching your instinctive nature.

LARRY: Do you trade instinctive? When you trade you'll buy and sell 3 or 4 times in a day.

LIN: No, I'll buy for the move and to me the move is going to happen within a week. It might me today, it might be 2 days, it might be 3 days or it might take all week. The move is either up or down: If I'm wrong it's down; if I'm right, it's up.

JOHN: O.K., because I've noticed correlations between people who to the degree to which they are dominant in the invent instinct, or recessively invent instinct, and how long they actually keep the trade. Tell me if this analogy sounds wrong: You're juggling the stocks in the air. You keep catching them, looking at them, saying do I keep willing to invest that money in that or shall I drop it? In other words, is this still where it's at for another period of time?

LARRY: No. That's wrong. Mine is has it got to my objective and should I get out yet. Do my rules say get out? It isn't an evaluating (this vs. that), it's: is it time to get out? Is the system telling me to get out?

LIN: I've really enjoyed this. I think we've really had some interesting wanderings here and yet there is a lot of interesting pieces of information. Thank you, Larry, for the information.

JOHN: I think one of the things that I'm beginning to understand is that there are essentially, from an instinctive point of view, two kinds of traders. At the first level, first tier, one kind of trader is the trader who trades in a very small way and I don't mean financially. I mean he either trades for himself, or they're a trader with a few clients and it's their advice that stems from their knowledge, their intuition, their whatever, their system, rather than an institution. . The traders who are not working for major institutions and are not working in collaboration with a whole team of people will be invent, which is why we have consistently seen the people who we've interviewed be dominant invent people. I think there are two sides to this whole thing. Well, sorry, let me say here, on that first thought: Those who work for an institution and who are institutional traders with major trading programs and things like that, those money managers, I think, will be more the order seek people because they're naturally inclined to work for institutions in the first place. They're not the kind of people who feel comfortable alone. I wrote some time ago that order and seek people find safety in numbers. So when there is a whole team consensus, and there is a body of knowledge, and a whole pattern to it, and there is a program literally written that will drive how the trades are done, that will be the order seek person.

LIN: Also, the people who are gut-feel like Larry and myself probably have a harder time having the public trust us because we're going with our gut. And to them that doesn't make as much sense as the guy who can tell you all his order and his rules and get comfortable with that.

JOHN: Absolutely, which is why reputation is such an enormous factor when people are looking for an individual like you or Larry for advice. They will look at your past record and say, "Well, we don't know quite how he does it, but whatever he does it seems to work, so we're going to trust him" and that's where the trust issue comes in. Now, let's go with the small people, the Linda's, the Larry's, the you's of the world who we've interviewed who are high in invent. They're high in invent, that's one category. Now there's a sub category within that which is really, really interesting. You don't have a second suit per se. You have such a strong dominance in invent, that you're whole style tends to be a gut-driven intuitive style. Larry does not have as much invent as you do and has a strong second suit in seek. So although he is an individual isolationist or an individual trader, he then uses a second suit which determines the fact that he looks at data and analysis in what he does following and backing up the gut. I think Linda was the one who has order—now I need to check on it—has order as a second suit and she was the one who tends to be more of a program kind of trader but on a very individual kind of basis. So there is almost like there is a category which is you're either invent, in which case you trade individually or you are order in which case you trade institutionally and then the sub category is if your second suit being in the invent group now, your second suit is seek, you'll be a complete data trader or an analysis or value trader or an order—sorry, the seek would be the analysis, data trader, the value trader is going to be the order kind of trader. Or if you're super high in invent, you're definitely going to be the absolute gut feel, feel-the-marketplace kind of trader. And I wonder what the second seek create would create in a trader? Maybe that's the person who goes wandering around and looks at pork bellies and things. I don't know. We need to look at that.

LIN: Well, there are people who will like...Peter Lynch says his wife goes to the market and she comes back and says, you know there's this wonderful new Hanes pantyhose display, or it's the Legs that comes in the shell and the packaging looks good, the people will...

JOHN: That probably is the create

LIN: And that's maybe create where they've thought it through and realized that there is some value that can be created by buying this.

JOHN: And I'll tell you what, you've just given me an idea. The create instinct needs to have quality in their life. They really look for things that are made of quality, that are quality in every aspect. So probably the high create second suit, in other words, invent create trader, is going to be the one who, yeah goes on gut, but looks for inherent quality in the products of the company's manufacturing because those are the ones which most defeat entropy which is the natural law of the universe that says everything that we create will, given time, try to reduce itself back the normal chaos or the breakdown of natural energy which is chaos.

LIN: And also, this person can take more risks because they can let something go against them that Larry and I wouldn't let go against us because we're looking at the price and we're saying, "It's going to go up and if it doesn't we'll take our loss." They, on the other hand, are looking at the price and they are looking at the quality and they're saying, "Well the quality is still there even though it's down." So they will take risk, in that sense, that they will allow it to go against them and if they're wrong, they will probably take a bigger loss.

JOHN: Could well be. It would be interesting to talk to someone who fits that profile. We don't have one yet. What we're really telling people in the book is that even if you're in the right place in terms of your high invent and you are attracted to this industry because of that and you're up on your analysis, this book will give you the confidence based on your Psychometric Test Result of following what it is that you know now you should do because most people fail through hesitation, not because they were going in the wrong direction. All is lost to he who fails. That line has been said so many times in so many different ways. The guy buys the book and says, "Gee, now I've never really won big, I've never really made it. These guys have. Let me read what they did." Well, without a doubt, without an exception, everyone of the people who have succeeded have the confidence not to hesitate and, as Larry told us just now, he learned at some point, sure enough there were things that he learned as a child which were important. And he also learned that there are a lot of people out there who were full of bull. They just didn't know what they were doing and he was looking to these other people because they had big mouths thinking they knew more. He realized, and he said it in the interview...

LIN: They were all older.

JOHN: And they were all older, and he...

LIN: He thought they had more experience.

JOHN: Right. And he realized...

LIN: That experience is not results.

JOHN: Exactly. And he realized that in order for him to succeed he just had to get up and do it himself and trust his own *method*. And that's really what we're saying to people: If you're high invent-seek and you've always wanted to use information and data, stop sitting on the sidelines and get active and that is the way you should be doing it. So we're just confirming people's inner feelings, and helping them direct that energy in the right way.

LIN: And also, if you're going to utilize the skills of others, this will allow you to understand what skills the other people have. If you know who you are and you know enough about how we're programmed, then you can also meet someone else, learn how they think and understand your broker better so that your broker...you can barter your skills. If you are high in order and low in invent and he's high in invent and low in order, you can work better.

JOHN: Absolutely. It will take away some of the ambiguity that people find in relationships with their traders and their brokers. The person who doesn't understand how his broker thinks or why he does things the way he does and forever is nervous and threatens to take his account somewhere else, will suddenly see the advantage of having that broker and will stop bugging him to start with. But secondly...

LIN: Will get a new broker.

JOHN: Or get a new broker. Yeah. Hey, this is not a comfortable way for me to be, given my instinctive nature and I just don't feel comfortable, and therefore I'm going to look

LIN: for someone who fits my profile better because that way I can enjoy this whole experience and be more involved.

LIN: How would you learn of the inherent discipline of your broker?

JOHN: Discipline, whether in trading or anything else, but in the context of the book—discipline is the conscious action with the conscious usage of mental energy which is counter-intuitive or counter-instinctive. It's directing us towards doing things that we would not naturally do. So it is a conscious directing of mental energy to create certain outcomes that we would not normally achieve if we were using our unconscious or our instinctive mental energy.

LIN: That is tantamount to saying that a person learns discipline and that is their instinctive path.

About the Author

Lin G. Eldridge

In 1963 I was hired by Shearson, Hammill and Co. (now Shearson/American Express) as a stockbroker in Palm Springs, California, and was trained in New York.

Having set a rapid production pace as a leader of a training class at age 22, in 1967 at age 26, I was sent again to New York to attend the first Shearson management-training program. Upon completion, I returned to the Los Angeles office as stockholder and office manager. Los Angeles was Shearson's third largest office behind Chicago and New York. (I turned the office from a group of turbulent prima donnas to a cadre of healthy, seasoned veterans who worked long hours and were loyal.) In 1969 I became involved in corporate finance and placed several major financings, and arranged the merger of Explorer Motor Homes into National Industries.

In early 1970 I left Shearson proud of my association and accepted a personal challenge of personal investments and managing individual accounts with a combined managed account of around $2 million by trading securities, which were primarily new corporate underwritings and OTC stocks. Working at home in Carmel, California, with a quote machine in my office, I was able to increase the value of my account and clients by over 500% in three years.

In 1970 I also became active in real estate, becoming licensed in California and forming partnerships to develop land into several residential communities in Monterey and Santa Barbara Counties, in addition to a major project in Lubbock, Texas. I was first employed in commercial real estate by Del Monte Properties in Monterey in 1970.

I formed Preferred Properties, a real estate company, in Carmel, California in 1975 and once again formed a cadre of professional workers, which evolved into an aggressive, profitable venture that I sold in 1980 to Century 21.

Trained as a "door opener" and "cold caller," I knocked on the door of every institutional type of real estate name in every high-rise in San Francisco, thereby finding out what the real market was for institutional property. The problem now was product! I sold a syndicator a $7,000,000 office building in Arlington, Texas and put together a group to buy development land, but feared that I needed direction and national support. In October of 1980, upon knocking on the door of Sierra R.E.I.T., I was referred to Arthur Rubloff & Co., who found in checking my references that the association was to be a "both win" situation. I later became a Vice President and top institutional salesman in 1981 and 1982. I arranged financing for the first phase of $9 million. This was the beginning of a $460 million project in Aurora, Colorado. This loan closed April 15, 1982. Financing is both construction and mini-permanent three years including participation of 50%.

From 1983-1984 I was a Vice President of Cushman & Wakefield and headed the new west coast mortgage brokerage department.

From 1984-1987 I was a private real estate broker and formed apartment partnerships, acting as General Partner in the San Francisco Bay area.

From 1988 to present I have been a private investor in Seattle, Washington, using fundamental and technical trading strategies which utilized options and stock equities. My portfolio increased in value over the last three years:

1991	155% Audited
1992	134% Audited
1993	65%

www.ingramcontent.com/pod-product-compliance
Lightning Source LLC
Chambersburg PA
CBHW031053180526
45163CB00002BA/817